THE BALLAD OF
RANGO™

THE ART & MAKING OF AN OUTLAW FILM

Foreword by GORE VERBINSKI Written by DAVID S. COHEN

INSIGHT EDITIONS

San Rafael, California

page 1: CRASH M^CCREERY ❧ *Rango Sheriff*
pages 2–3: ILM ❧ *Final Render*
pages 4–5: ILM ❧ *Final Render*
right: CRASH M^CCREERY ❧ *"Where are your friends now, amigo?"*
following pages: ILM ❧ *Final Render*

Library of Congress Cataloging-in-Publication Data available.

ISBN: 978-1-60887-017-2

ROOTS of PEACE   🌲 REPLANTED PAPER

Insight Editions, in association with Roots of Peace, will plant
two trees for each tree used in the manufacturing of this book.
Roots of Peace is an internationally renowned humanitarian
organization dedicated to eradicating land mines worldwide and
converting war-torn lands into productive farms and wildlife
habitats. Together, we will plant two million fruit and nut trees
in Afghanistan and provide farmers there with the skills and
support necessary for sustainable land use.

Manufactured in China by Insight Editions

10 9 8 7 6 5 4 3 2 1

INSIGHT 👁 EDITIONS
10 Paul Drive
San Rafael, CA 94903
www.insighteditions.com

CONTENTS

FOREWORD

BEFORE THERE WAS SOUP, there was the primordial vapor: shapeless, without form. Just an idea rummaging around the frontal lobe. I am in awe of the process by which gas becomes solid, ideas become image. When concepts are rendered, a language is developed and from that language, a voice. If I could sit around a fire and tell a story, you would imagine it in your own way. The artist renders his own imagination. It is a wondrous process of creation, and when you work with virtuosos, it is a privilege to observe.

The cast of characters that collaborated on this film were misfits. With all our collective experience, we remained inexperienced: naïve and yet blindly optimistic. Having never made an animated film before, we were somehow liberated from convention. We simply never thought of the film as "animated"—as if that word implied some "type" or "genre." Any limitations we encountered only seemed to inspire the tribe to continue forward with an explorer's instinct. Drawn toward the unknown.

Live-action filmmaking is like wielding a butterfly net. One orchestrates conflict and stands poised, ready to capture the moment of truth. In animation, there is no "real time." Only fragments, created and bundled to depict "real time." Therefore, we had to fabricate the anomaly. We were in constant pursuit of the "awkward moment." The creation and the preservation of it. This was our mantra. And the artists gave a performance in honor of that belief. As they conjured, the story began to evolve. The Muse began to play that string between their minds and their fingers. Strange things began to happen.

From its inception, *Rango* was always an identity quest: the chameleon discovering who he is. Gas becoming matter. So too was the journey of the film itself. I am honored to have had the opportunity to work with such a brilliant group of artists. These images are their words. This is their story: *The Ballad of Rango*.

—GORE VERBINSKI

PART I
RANCHO RANGO

SOMETHING NEW

IT'S A SPARKLING summer day in Southern California's San Fernando Valley, and on the patio outside his office, Gore Verbinski has found a rare moment to enjoy the breeze. This second-floor sanctuary has as serene a vista as a busy studio lot can offer: a tidy golf course just across the concrete channel of the Los Angeles River. The calm is misleading. Verbinski's deadline to deliver *Rango* is just four months away, and nearly all of his waking hours are consumed with the hundred labors he must complete to finish the movie.

Verbinski has worked under pressure before. He directed the first *Pirates of the Caribbean* trilogy, with its huge budgets and enormous stakes for the entire Walt Disney Company. This movie is something different though, something more personal: a vision lovingly crafted by a talented team of artists, then nurtured and protected by Verbinski so as to honor their initial creative vision.

"I believe that audiences are always hungry for something new, something truly original," he says thoughtfully. "You sit in a big theater, and you go, 'Oh, that was a little weird,' or 'Well, that was different!' All those bumps and flaws and choices, that's voice. And I just love movies that have a voice. So much of what we do is about elimination of voice. We need to find that moment that's just a little awkward, a little off, and celebrate it, put a magnifying glass on it, champion it. I've been lucky enough to surround myself with very talented artists who I think also believe the same thing."

Something new, something daring: many filmmakers dream of making such a movie. As artists, filmmakers are drawn to novelty and experimentation, but their instincts are often tempered by a Hollywood machine that likes to grind down any project's sharp edges.

After the success of the *Pirates* trilogy, Verbinski didn't succumb to the Hollywood lure and continue making blockbusters. He pivoted instead to an animated feature—his first—about a narcissistic chameleon with an identity crisis. To create a unique tone and look, he enlisted a cadre of trusted artists and nurtured them in a cloistered workspace where their ideas could flourish. He persuaded Industrial Light & Magic, the visual effects giant George Lucas founded to make *Star Wars*, to create the digital animation for the entire movie, something that ILM had never done. Each choice was designed to ensure *Rango* really *would* be something new.

Ironically, this moviemaking adventure was born in classic Hollywood fashion: a pitch meeting at an old showbiz haunt, Art's Deli in Studio City.

Verbinski had been invited there by two old friends, David Shannon and John Carls, before the first *Pirates* film went into production. Shannon was a successful writer and illustrator of children's books and a close friend of Verbinski's. Carls was a producer with roots in both live-action and animation. Verbinski had worked briefly with both men on separate occasions: with Carls in the late 1990s trying to make a movie of Maurice Sendak's *Where the Wild Things Are*, and with Shannon on an attempt to develop a movie version of one of Shannon's books.

Shannon and Carls had been batting around ideas for an animated movie, finally settling on Carls's notion of a

Western, set in the desert, with desert animals for the characters. Now Carls wanted Verbinski to direct it. Live-action directors rarely try directing animation, as the animation production is quite unlike live-action, but Carls knew his man. Verbinski had worked with animation on commercials and music videos (the animated Budweiser Frogs spots had launched him into features), and Carls was sure he had the right instincts. "He storyboarded all his films," says Carls, "so he understood that initial stage of the animation process."

Verbinski's offbeat sensibility also fit the project, which hoped to break the smooth-and-sunny mold of most American animation. "We're all fans of movies that have a little bit of a dark edge to them and a sort of an oddball sense of humor," says Shannon. "Just a little bit twisted."

The pitch from Carls and Shannon was just a seed, really, but Verbinski liked it and agreed to help nurture it. Going for a fish-out-of-water story, the trio made a lost pet chameleon their hero. Shannon gave him a resemblance to Don Knotts. "I'm a big fan of Don Knotts," he says, "and we pictured [our chameleon] as that kind of character."

Since their story would be set in the desert and many chameleons are tropical rainforest dwellers, they decided the plot should revolve around water. Shannon began generating concept art and character drawings. "We just started to spitball," says Shannon. "We were just looking through books of animals from the desert, going 'Oh, y'know, we gotta have a tortoise. We could have a rattlesnake for a bad guy.'"

But one *Pirates* movie became three, and months became years. *Rango* simmered on everyone's back burner, though the idea didn't die. Verbinski and Shannon would kick the idea around over breakfasts and at "streamside meetings" on fishing trips.

The years on *Pirates* gave Verbinski the chance to add another indispensable attachment: Johnny Depp, whom he wanted as the voice of Rango. "There was always only one choice," says Verbinski. "In my mind, it had to be Johnny Depp. I designed the character for him from the outset." A movie meant to be as eccentric as *Rango* would need Depp's star power. In fact, without Depp, Verbinski might have dropped the project—but on hearing the pitch, says Verbinski, Depp "was in immediately."

pages 10–11: ILM ❧ *Final Render*
preceding pages: CHRISTIAN ALZMANN & JOHN BELL ❧ *The Posse Looks Out*
left: ILM ❧ *Final Render*

ASSEMBLING THE ENSEMBLE

ONCE DONE WITH *Pirates 3*, director Gore Verbinski wasted no time getting *Rango* back underway. He invited screenwriter and playwright John Logan, whose credits included such epics as *The Aviator* and *Gladiator*, to work on the script. Somewhat to Verbinski's surprise, Logan was excited by the idea. "My great passion in life is the desert and hiking in the desert," says Logan. "And I've never written a Western, so doing something different is always exciting to any writer, particularly to me."

Independent producer Graham King, who'd recently won the Best Picture Oscar for *The Departed*, agreed to put up some seed money, and Verbinski asked another friend, producer Adam Cramer, to write up a rough budget. Cramer had worked with Verbinski on music videos in the mid-1980s, and they'd been close ever since. Once the budget was complete, Verbinski coaxed Cramer to stay on as a producer.

With resources for work to start in earnest, Verbinski was determined to make something truly unconventional. "I am a fan of the flawed movie," he says. "Perfection is the wrong goal. You want to pursue the singularities that make film unique; find the moment that is a little awkward, a little off, and celebrate it—put a magnifying glass on it.

Yet to distinguish his movie he knew he'd have to nurture it in isolation, and on a relative shoestring. "With money comes

above: A wall in Gore Verbinski's office at Rancho Rango

opinions, and with opinions comes a narrowing of voice," he says. "It's very important to create a bubble and a sort of sanctuary where you can just work on the canvas."

Physically, that sanctuary would be Verbinski's former home in the hills below the Angeles National Forest, which he keeps as a retreat. There his group would craft a story and script, discover the picture's look, and assemble a story reel to serve as both the pitch to studios and, eventually, a template for animators. The house was soon dubbed Rancho Rango.

The team began to form in the fall of 2007. Writer and illustrator David Shannon returned as producer, working mainly from his home studio but coming over with art twice a week or so. Next to join was James Ward Byrkit, a storyboard artist who'd worked on most of Verbinski's movies. "I get the call," says Byrkit, "and he says, 'Can you come over? Because I have this super top-secret project going I want to tell you about.' I knew it must be the animated thing."

Verbinski's pitch, "which was just this scramble in his brain," left Byrkit laughing so hard he was convinced the movie would work. Though he had been in line for TV directing work, that night he told his wife, "I think I'm gonna stop these other [projects]." Soon Byrkit was working at the house full-time, drawing on the dining room table. He would eventually become *Rango*'s head of story.

Another recruit was storyboard artist and children's book writer Eugene Yelchin, who'd worked alongside Verbinski early in both their careers. *Rango* was perfect for Yelchin; his own books had animal characters, and he'd become a connoisseur of Westerns after seeing *The Magnificent Seven* as a boy in Leningrad. "I was obsessed with cowboys and Westerns for years and years, before I switched to rock 'n' roll," he says.

The fourth artist to sign up was creature designer Mark "Crash" McCreery, who'd conjured the squid-bearded Davy Jones for the *Pirates* movies. "His work is so highly detailed blood flows through it. It actually starts to lift off the page," Verbinski says. McCreery became *Rango*'s production designer.

Verbinski gave the group great freedom to explore. "I don't think you impose a style upon a film," he says. "I think a film tells you what the style needs to be, and it sort of grows out of that. And in the case of *Rango*, it is an identity quest, somebody who's searching for who he is. The film is very much doing the same thing. So right from the outset, it was clear that this film had to find its own language, its own style."

JIM BYRKIT

DIRECTOR GORE VERBINSKI CALLS HIS RELATIONSHIP with head of story Jim Byrkit "absolutely symbiotic." He relies on Byrkit as a sounding board for hammering out problems, sometimes acting out scenes with him to spot writing problems. "We've just worked together so long that we kind of finish each other's sentences," Verbinski says.

Besides generating thousands of drawings and serving as head of story, Byrkit was Verbinski's session partner for composing the early versions of songs for the Mariachi Owls, *Rango*'s Mexican Greek Chorus. "It was a very lean process," recalls Byrkit. "With such a small group of talented guys, everyone had to do many jobs. Gore and I would be recording a song while [producer] Adam [Cramer] was in the kitchen sculpting and [production designer] Crash [McCreery] was cranking out unbelievable artwork on the other side of the wall."

Verbinski and Byrkit also did most of the character voices for the original story reel. That made it a struggle to keep each character distinct. "That's when the ridiculous would really take over," says Byrkit. "Gore and I would try out new lines, saying the most absurd things to get the other guy to laugh. [Screenwriter] John Logan even joined in a few times—he plays an excellent villain. Those days were nonstop creative bliss." ☻

top: JIM BYRKIT ✧ *Original Elgin Sketch*
right: JIM BYRKIT ✧ *Original Rango Hero Sketch*

With that freedom, though, came a challenge for the group. "Our enemy is not a person or a system," Verbinski told them. "Our enemy is mediocrity. It's a force like gravity. It wears on you and you have to constantly fight back against it, resist its pull." Verbinski asked them to work without fear and gave them a space where it was safe to make mistakes along the way.

Paradoxically, that put the onus on Verbinski to provide firm guidance, lest precious time and resources be wasted on fruitless experiments. *Rango*'s look was to be inspired by old Westerns, especially the spaghetti Westerns of Sergio Leone, with their tense staredowns and standoffs. Leone's pictures and other Westerns were played continuously on the flatscreen in the living room so that look would be constantly in the artists' minds.

The character designs would combine iconic Western characters with desert animals. Yelchin explains, "For example, there's always a gambler in those saloon scenes in the West.

What is it about the gambler's ability to see things that I respond to? I put an owl in that role, because the owl can turn his head 180 degrees. It's finding psychology out of form."

Verbinski told the artists to focus on personality as they designed the characters and demanded bold silhouettes, so each of the hundred-plus characters—many more than usual in an animated movie—would be distinct. The sets would be designed in the same spirit. The animals' town of Dirt would have the silhouette of a classic Western-movie town but be built from human detritus: the saloon is made from a gas can, the post office from an old metal mailbox, and so on.

Notably, of the core group on *Rango*, only producer John Carls had ever made an animated movie. But as often as it was pointed out to the filmmakers, the lack of experience in this medium never hindered the process. "We were always making a movie, the fact that it was an animated movie never really changed our approach to telling the story," says Verbinski.

above left: Eugene Yelchin
above right: Jim Byrkit

"[We realized] the only way we're going to succeed is to do what we know and hope it translates," says McCreery. They knew how to make a good movie; they would just be making their movie in an unfamiliar way.

The group at Rancho Rango grew. Concept artist James Carson came on to create sets and environments. One of Carson's first drawings helped set the look for Dirt. "It has this starkness—very rich, deep colors and a lot of contrast [and] shadows—and everyone seemed very pleased with it," he says. "Once that had been established, we just carried that visual theme throughout."

More story artists came in to help Verbinksi and Byrkit build the story reel, including David Feiss and Jurgen Gross. Film editor Wyatt Jones worked with a lone assistant in one room— unless Verbinski and Byrkit wanted to record dialogue for the story reel, in which case that room became an impromptu recording studio. Music editor Ken Karman and his assistant Jeannie Lee Marks worked on

a temporary score, some of which was incorporated into *Rango*'s final music.

Research trips were an important part of the work. Some were as simple as an early trip to a pet store, where a chameleon whose bulging eyes reminded them of Don Knotts had the group chortling. Later, on a trip to Joshua Tree National Park, they were inspired by a late-day encounter with some drooping cacti. "They had these accidental faces through their spines kind of coming down," says McCreery. "There was so much character in these things. In a regal kind of way, they were like the guardians of where we were and they were watching us and you didn't want to do anything wrong around them. Gore [Verbinski] said, 'I think these are the spirits of the West.'" They became *Rango*'s Cactus Spirits.

The vibe at Rancho Rango was just as stimulating. "It was kind of an outlaw atmosphere," remembers Shannon. Friday barbecues built camaraderie and kept morale up. Foosball in the living room and bocce ball out back gave everyone a chance to stretch and decompress. "I think blood flow has a tremendous amount to do with the creative process," says Verbinski.

above left: Cactus Spirits reference photography
above right: Crash McCreery and Gore Verbinski
left: DAVID SHANNON ✣ *Bar Fly*

CRASH McCREERY

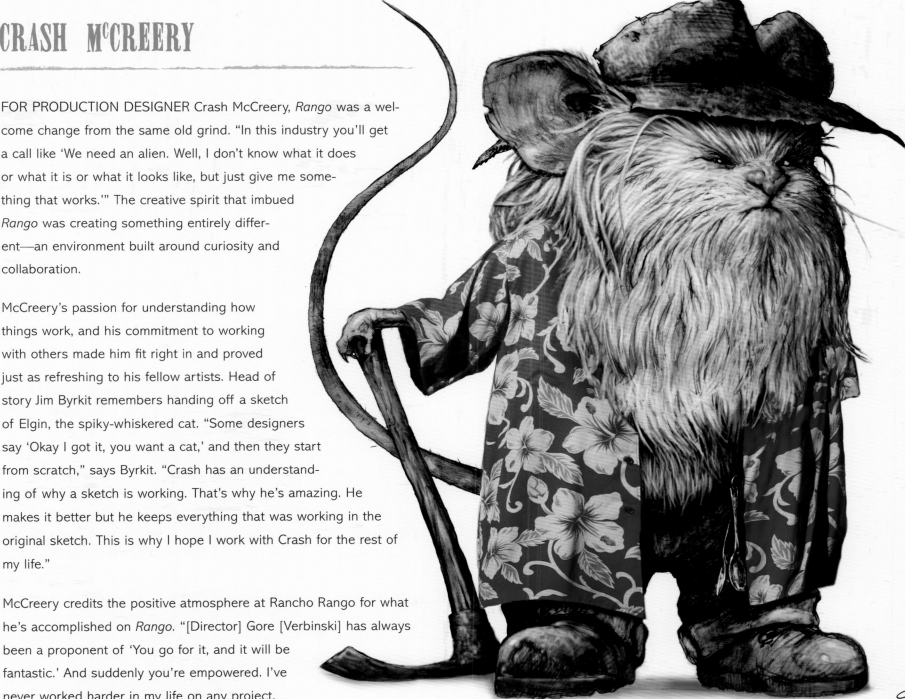

FOR PRODUCTION DESIGNER Crash McCreery, *Rango* was a welcome change from the same old grind. "In this industry you'll get a call like 'We need an alien. Well, I don't know what it does or what it is or what it looks like, but just give me something that works.'" The creative spirit that imbued *Rango* was creating something entirely different—an environment built around curiosity and collaboration.

McCreery's passion for understanding how things work, and his commitment to working with others made him fit right in and proved just as refreshing to his fellow artists. Head of story Jim Byrkit remembers handing off a sketch of Elgin, the spiky-whiskered cat. "Some designers say 'Okay I got it, you want a cat,' and then they start from scratch," says Byrkit. "Crash has an understanding of why a sketch is working. That's why he's amazing. He makes it better but he keeps everything that was working in the original sketch. This is why I hope I work with Crash for the rest of my life."

McCreery credits the positive atmosphere at Rancho Rango for what he's accomplished on *Rango*. "[Director] Gore [Verbinski] has always been a proponent of 'You go for it, and it will be fantastic.' And suddenly you're empowered. I've never worked harder in my life on any project, and I don't think I've done better work on any project in my life. And I think it's for that reason." 🟡

above: CRASH McCREERY ✧ *Spoons Hawaiian Color Design*

A MUSICAL ROMANTIC

"I'M A FAILED MUSICIAN," laments director Gore Verbinski. "Music is my love, and I'm just not good enough to make a living at it." He keeps a pair of electric guitars at the ready in his office and his regular jam sessions with head of story Jim Byrkit provided fodder for *Rango*'s score.

Music editor Ken Karman came on early at Rancho Rango but notes, "It was not too early for Gore [Verbinski] to want to start experimenting with music and specifically experimenting with this notion of the mariachi Greek chorus that follows our hero through the film."

Karman calls Verbinski "romantic" when it comes to music. "He's not interested in things being polished per se. He just wants them to be authentic. He doesn't want to just go get a nice new take of something and move on. He wants to reach in there, pull it inside out and dissect it, then put it back together and see what happens."

Karman calls the use of music in *Rango* "quirky and very idiosyncratic," adding, "I think the final film will be as surprising for where there isn't music as where there is. And I think that some of it will be completely out in left field." ◉

right: DAVID SHANNON ⬩ *Banjo Rat*

"If you sit in one place and try to crack a problem, quite often you'll have blockage. But if you start to move, solutions inevitably present themselves."

When it came to the art, teamwork ruled. Byrkit and the other story artists would hand off character drawings to McCreery, who'd "Crash-ify" them, as the team came to call it, adding detail, texture, and "fuzz" (see Page 126 for more on this notion of "fuzz").

THE SPIRIT QUEST

WHILE THE ARTISTS were creating *Rango*'s look, director Gore Verbinski, head of story Jim Byrkit, and writer John Logan were turning the concept into a script. Logan would arrive at the house in shorts with a hydration pack, ready to talk story on a long ramble in the hills.

To Logan, the project felt like a freewheeling adventure. "I don't know if there's a story there. Can we be this surreal in an animated movie? All of it was done with just that sense of rolling the dice crazily." He admits feeling like a tweed-jacketed professor dropped into a nest of crazy artists, and in fact Verbinski calls Logan "The Professor," the man who kept the story on track. He credits Logan with helping them remember "the plot is completely secondary to the character's quest. It's about identity. It's about *who is he*? Once we discovered the course of our narrative, all this sort of dream logic began to bubble up to the surface. The simplicity of the quest allowed for abstractions."

The trio decided—boldly, given that talking-animal movies tend to be children's fare—not to shy from scary, dark, or just plain weird moments. "Gore [Verbinski] loves the surreality of the desert," says Byrkit, "so we knew that Rango's going to go on a spiritual quest and find odd things in the desert. We knew this was a playground for the imagination and a way to express psychological states in a kids' movie."

above: Jim Byrkit and Gore Verbinski

THE STORY REEL

Every shot of Rango started as a black-and-white sketch, which was scanned and inserted into a timeline of the animatic or story reel, the final blueprint for the film. Many shots needed multiple frames and layers, or required several alternates, resulting in tens of thousands of individual drawings. "It was inspiring getting to work with a variety of story artists playing at the top of their game," says head of story Jim Byrkit. "One look at the style differences gives you a sense of the personalities of the guys. Everyone added a unique flavor to the stew."

The mix of talent brought together storyboard artists from live-action and story artists from animation, which are very different disciplines. Live-action storyboard artists are used to focusing on camera angles and movement in a scene, but not the acting—actors take care of that. Rango's storyboard artists had to learn to think like animation story artists, whose drawings lay the foundation for the performances animators create later on. Similarly, the animation artists had to adjust to director Gore Verbinski's demand for composition and construction of shots. The group would share their drawings freely—illustrator and producer David Shannon remembers lots of "oohs and ahs." The art inspired the writing even as the script shaped the art. ✪

above: DAVID FEISS ↯ *Hawk Escape Storyboards*

below: DAVID LOWERY ↯ *Let's Ride*

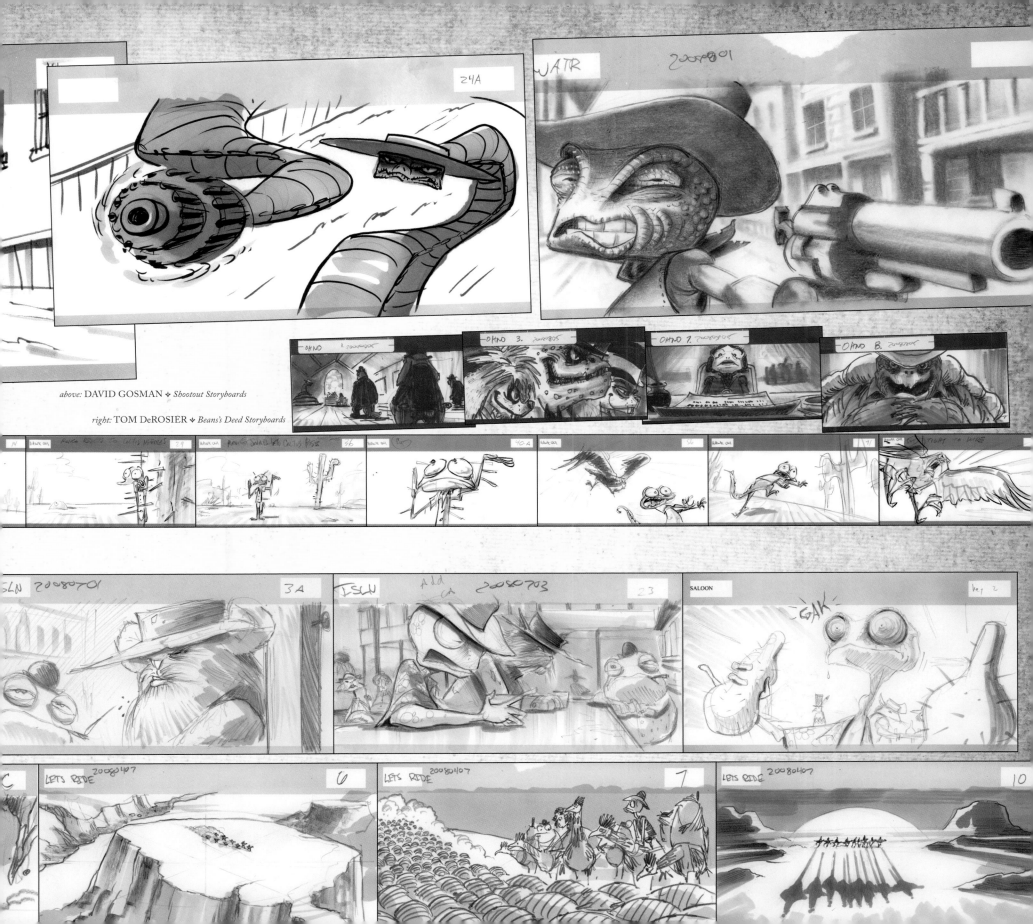

above: DAVID GOSMAN ↴ *Shootout Storyboards*

right: TOM DeROSIER ↴ *Beans's Deed Storyboards*

DESIGNING THE LEADS

THE CHARACTER DESIGN of the chameleon hero was settled—more or less—quite early, based on drawings by illustrator and producer David Shannon and head of story Jim Byrkit. The wide range of the performance the little chameleon would have to give, though, meant that getting the basics down wasn't enough. "When you're doing story-boards," says production designer Crash McCreery, "there are cheats left and right. But when it comes time to design one image that represents all of the storyboard moments, that's a challenge because there were just some outlandish stretches, and great liberty was taken." Since *Rango* would be animated in a realistic style, the character wouldn't be able to do all the "squashing and stretching" common in animation. "That was the bane of my existence for a while," says McCreery.

Byrkit had also proposed a "counterintuitive" idea: giving Rango tiny eyes in the middle of big green orbs, like the chameleon they'd seen in the pet store. "Usually, if you're doing an animated movie, you give the characters huge eyes, because they're expressive, and you can see them even when they're far away," he says. "The eye would be a big white ball with a big iris in the middle of it.

"I was proposing these very small eyes, but I said, 'That's okay, because the entire ball that they're wedged in is going to sort of become the eye. This whole ball will be expressive.'" Byrkit's idea carried the day.

While Rango's basic look was set early, the look of his love interest, Miss Beans, proved maddeningly elusive. "We just couldn't find her," says Byrkit. Shannon first imagined "Lillibelle" as a chubby toad, to contrast with Rango. Later she got a Goth look, with a bob hairstyle and a flat-brimmed black hat. That didn't stick, either. Byrkit says, "For months and months, Crash and I went back and forth trying to hone Beans. We would get close, but then it wouldn't quite be right. She would be too pretty or she would be too weird." At one point Beans was even a mammal, but the idea of a mammal-reptile romance proved queasy.

right: JIM BYRKIT ↳ *Early Fancy Sheriff Sketch*

PARAMOUNT: A HOME IN THE HIGH COUNTRY

AS THE STORY REEL neared completion, it was time to add another producer to work with digital animation. The choice was Shari Hanson, a veteran visual effects producer who'd spent years at Industrial Light & Magic and had most recently worked on the reboot of *Star Trek*.

"I just really fell in love with the character and the story," says Hanson. "I saw some initial drawings and illustrations of the Rango character, and he was just really sweet and lovable. There were several other character illustrations, and one in particular, [the illustration of] Gordy, one of the characters in the saloon . . . was so close to photorealism I knew immediately this was unlike any other animated feature."

Hanson, who tempers a producer's firm hand with a sunny disposition, was well familiar with photorealistic digital effects. But she admits joining the group was "pretty intimidating." Happily, though, she was prepared for that.

"Every film . . . is a family that gets thrown together at a moment in time and creates something together," she says, "so it's not an unfamiliar feeling [for] me." This was her first time working with director Gore Verbinski, though, and she was joining a team that had already been at work for months. It was a difficult situation for any producer. Nonetheless, she says, "they were fantastic about being open and accepting a new person into their team. And we had a lot of fun together." She visited Rancho Rango once or twice a week while beginning to set up the more formal offices that would host the production's next stage.

After nearly a year, the story reel was done, the characters designed, the art ready for a formal pitch. Invitations went out to the studios, and a parade of executives journeyed to the hills. They saw part of the story reel, heard Verbinski act out the story, and listened as head of story Jim Byrkit described *Rango*'s unique look.

"Paramount's response was the most enthusiastic," remembers Verbinski. "Brad Grey believed in *Rango* and in me. That trust allowed us to maintain relative autonomy throughout the process. Also, Paramount's marketing had a proven track record and the partnership with Nickelodeon felt synergistic."

In the autumn of 2008, as the economy was turning downward, Paramount Pictures stepped up and bought *Rango*. In November, the development team decamped from Rancho Rango and moved to more regular offices, where the little lizard found a new home.

The next step was to bring him to life. ✷

right: JIM BYRKIT ⬥ *Early Rango Expression Test*

PART II

ON THE RANGE

ILM JOINS UP

RANCHO RANGO HAD fostered a camaraderie and trust the core group of artists had come to cherish. Director Gore Verbinski wanted to preserve that same feeling as *Rango* moved into animation production, and he had his eye on a company he trusted to deliver *Rango*'s look in computer-generated (CG) animation. The problem was, it wasn't an animation studio.

Industrial Light & Magic, George Lucas's San Francisco–based visual effects giant, is the most famous visual effects (VFX) company in the world. Its list of credits includes most of the groundbreaking VFX movies of recent times, from *Star Wars* to *Jurassic Park* to *Avatar*. ILM had done the visual effects for Verbinski's *Pirates* trilogy, and the *Pirates 2* team of John Knoll, Hal Hickel, Charles Gibson, and Allen Hall had won the Best Visual Effects Oscar in 2007, in no small measure due to the photo-realistic animated characters of Davy Jones and his crew.

Verbinski wanted Knoll, Hickel, and ILM to apply their skills to *Rango*. ILM, however, was a visual effects company, and it had never done an animated feature. That, ironically, was exactly why Verbinski wanted them: "We were entering a field with no trodden path. We were able to make our own; we had to. I am not interested in a formula or a recipe. I'm focused on talent. I had completed thousands of shots at ILM. If there was a language, it was one of camaraderie as we moved into the unknown."

Getting ILM to sign on, though, took some convincing. Knoll remembers feeling tepid about the idea when Verbinski invited him to look at *Rango* art in the summer of 2007. "I really admire what a company like Pixar does. I think it's really beautiful," he says. "But I think of myself more as a live-action guy."

Knoll nevertheless agreed to the meeting, expecting to bow out even if ILM somehow took the project. But after seeing the art and hearing the pitch, he left thinking, "Oh my God, this stuff's fantastic. The character designs are amazing. I really want to see these guys move."

Knoll also saw an opportunity for his own company. *Rango*, with its photo-realistic look and dozens of characters, would force ILM to sharpen its tools for digital character animation, an ever more important part of the VFX business. With Knoll and Hickel in support, ILM brass agreed to bid for *Rango,* and the visual effects studio was officially on board before work ended at the house.

preceding pages: CRASH M^CCREERY ❧ *Posse Lineup*
left: ILM & ROGER DEAKINS ❧ *Hero Lighting Test*

"Many studios were questioning why I was adamant about using ILM and not a traditional animation studio," remembers Verbinksi. "Ultimately, supporting this decision required a leap of faith—faith in my decision-making process, in me not just as a director but as a producer."

ILM animators get to do emotive characters now and then, but they're more often asked to set blimps or trains in motion. They typically focus on the action in individual shots. Doing an animated feature and animating characters and creating scenes, though, would require a whole different approach. "Moving ILM from the mentality of 'the shot' to the mentality of 'the scene' was essential to the process," recalls Verbinski. "We had to become one. They were our partners in the narrative. Every discussion became about context."

For ILM animators, *Rango* represented an opportunity to flex their creativity, to become more complete partners in creating an entire film. So when Hal Hickel gathered the animators and asked who'd like to work on an all-animated movie, it was a stampede. "This is kind of a dream come true for a lot of us," says Jakub Pistecky, who wound up as lead animator for *Rango*'s villains. "Hands went diving into the air." Later, the handpicked *Rango* team gathered to meet Verbinski, see the designs, and hear him take them through the story. Says Knoll, "People were really enchanted. You could feel the wonder."

The two-dimensional character drawings soon became three-dimensional figures. But before those characters could play scenes, they needed voices. ⊛

left: ILM ❧ *Final Renders*

NETTING NUGGETS: RECORDING THE CAST

THERE'S A TRUISM among actors: "Acting is reacting." Alas, voice actors on animated films rarely get anything to react to. Typically they record their lines alone in a booth, reading from the script, perhaps with the director reading the other roles. The voice cast may never meet until they pose for photos at the red-carpet premiere.

For *Rango*, though, director Gore Verbinski wanted a completely different approach. He'd gather his actors on a soundstage to play scenes together and record them as a group, just as he might record dialogue while shooting live-action footage. He'd shoot video for the animators to use as reference, but there would be only enough sets, props, and costumes to help the cast get into character. The important thing was that the actors would have other actors to react to.

"In live-action," says Verbinski, "we use a camera like a butterfly net. You're pursuing the awkward moment or a little piece of chaos that you hope to capture. Those are the golden nuggets that you can build your movie around. The performances that were unexpected, that weren't cerebral, when something happened that forced an intuitive response. That's the magic."

For most roles, Verbinski pursued actors he might cast to play the role if they had to appear on screen: Ned Beatty for the Mayor; Isla Fisher for Rango's love interest, Beans; Abigail Breslin for little Priscilla; Harry Dean Stanton for the blind preacher, Balthazar.

The cast gathered in January 2009 for three weeks of "emotion capture." Some soon found themselves, as Fisher puts it, "discombobulated."

"I think they felt silly at first and a little naked," says Verbinski, and not everything came out of the group clean enough to use. Alfred Molina, the voice of armadillo-mystic Roadkill, remembers, "Gore Verbinski said at one point, 'Don't worry about being word-perfect, because we're going to rerecord the voices anyway." The actors would perform scenes with full movement, recorded on audio and video, then, if necessary, record again in a more traditional isolation booth, which was readily available and immediately adjacent on the stage.

But Fisher says playing scenes together still helped, even in the iso-booth. "Once you physicalize the action of a scene, you still have the electricity of the fear in your body if it's a scary scene or the adrenaline from a love scene."

Head of story Jim Byrkit, who had no acting credits, found himself voicing five characters, including the significant supporting role of Waffles—something he found far more challenging than creating art. "Waffles talks in a loud whisper all the time," he says ruefully. "I can do that for about five minutes before I lose my voice. And Gore [Verbinski] makes you do take after take after take. You're standing there with Johnny Depp or Isla Fisher, and you can just feel you've only got three minutes left. And then two, and then one, and then your voice is gone. That was tough."

But Byrkit also understood that the goal was to get what Verbinski calls "fuzz." "Gore says, 'put some fuzz on it.' That means mess it up a little bit. Don't make it so perfect. Don't make it so clean. In reality, people stumble. We were always aware of trying to add those little unexpected tweaks or quirks or oddities that make it sound special." ❂

above: (left to right) Stephen Root, Ian Abercrombie, Jim Byrkit, Blake Clark, Lew Temple, John Cothran, Alex Manugian

left: (left to right) Martin Schaer, Stephen Root, Gil Birmingham, Ian Abercrombie, Jim Byrkit, Lew Temple, John Cothran, Alex Manugian, Gore Verbinski

ANIMATING THE CHARACTERS

RANGO HAS MORE than one hundred characters based on dozens of distinct desert creatures. ILM's animators and creature department are used to trying to simulate reality, but their mandate on *Rango* was to create characters first and animals second. "[Production designer] Crash [McCreery] would always be telling us, 'Don't try to make it about something in real life,'" says model supervisor Geoff Campbell. "It's all about getting into the feel of these characters."

Building functioning digital models was a challenge, too. Computer-animated characters are operated like puppets, with controls for every feature and limbs that must move or flex for the desired performance. For *Rango*, ILM had to develop a new way of building "rigging," which gives each character its skeleton and controls, so the characters could give nuanced performances.

ILM's animators also had to become better actors. Their early efforts were rejected for being too bouncy, too lively, and Kevin Martel, lead animator for the chameleon hero, says the whole animation team had to rethink their approach. "We get scenes with this crazy dialogue and these bananas characters, we're excited, and the tendency is to go overboard. You just want to do everything. It's like playing music where there's a certain time to solo and there's another time you've got to kind of lay back, and it's this guy's turn to solo. But we were all soloing." They had to learn a more subtle performance style, as well as a slower rhythm that reflected the Sergio Leone influence, says McCreery. "Tension is built by what's not going on. I think that kind of permeated this show. We had to take it down, take it way down, so when something is said or when something pops, it really means something, so it's not just this barrage of funny antics and slapstick humor."

The animators are the actors, and director Gore Verbinski spoke to them as actors, not as technicians. "Don't be afraid to do nothing," he would say. "Don't be afraid of the awkward pause or hesitation. We need to find that little flicker in the eye that says doubt. If Rango has doubts, don't telegraph it." In the case of marking a moment, he would often have the animators accentuate a preceding action and then abruptly stop. "When the smile fades, that's the moment. You don't need to fabricate it."

The payoff came as the first tests trickled in from ILM. "It was love at first sight," says producer Shari Hanson. "You just instantly love the character, love how he looks, love how sort of flawed but unique he is." Head of story Jim Byrkit remembers, "It was like Christmas," adding, "There was this wave of presents coming in. You've been drawing him for two years, and in your mind you know how he talks and you know how he moves, but you don't know if it's achievable. In movies you're so used to seeing the final product come back and be less than you were hoping. But when ILM delivered these few shots and it was everything we hoped, a wave of gratitude took us over." ✺

above left: ILM & CRASH M^cCREERY ✹ *Paint on Final Rango Render*
opposite (clockwise from top left): ADAM CRAMER ✹ *Rango Sculpture;*
ADAM CRAMER ✹ *Rango Sculpture;* ILM ✹ *Early Models after Render;*
Adam Cramer at work on Rattlesnake Jake Sculpture; ADAM CRAMER ✹
Rango Sculpture; ADAM CRAMER ✹ *Beans Sculpture*

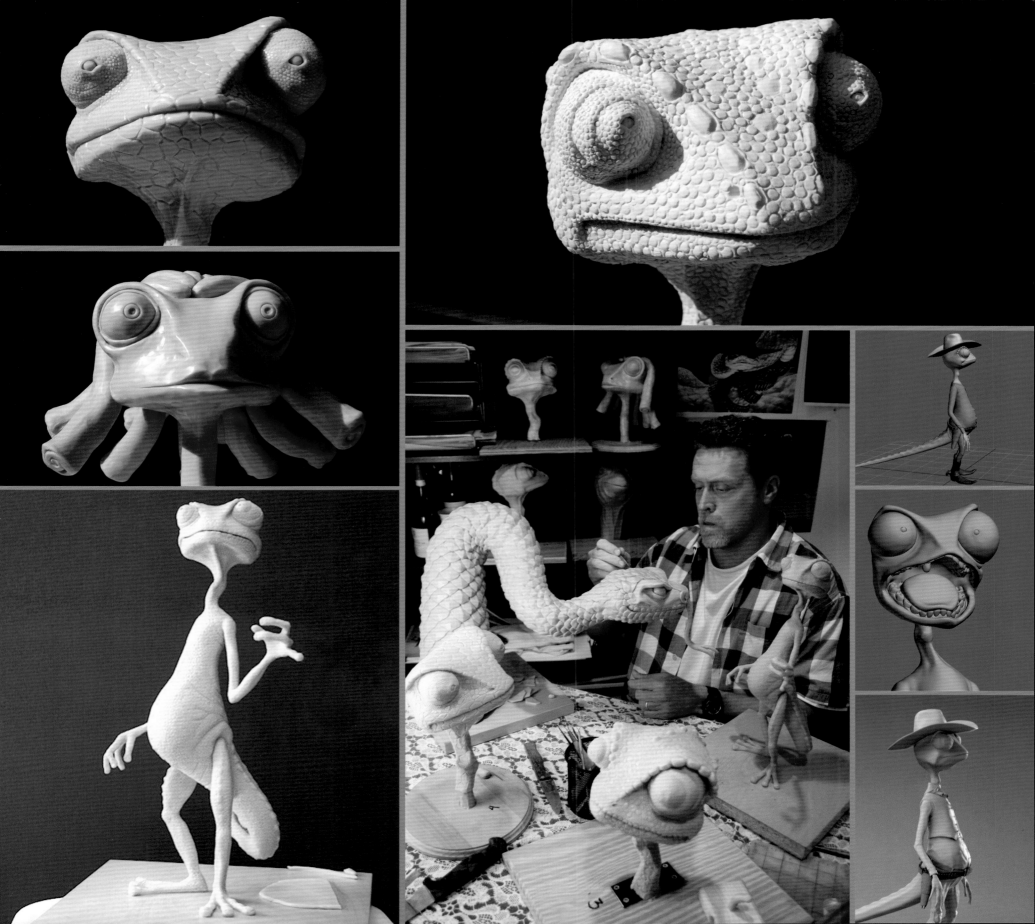

RANGO

———— ★ ————

"**R**ANGO'S WORLD IS LITERALLY SHATTERED IN THE FIRST TWO MINUTES OF THE MOVIE," SAYS WRITER JOHN LOGAN, "AND HE HAS TO REBUILD IT."

Our hero is a natural actor—he *is* a chameleon, after all—but doesn't know who he truly is. He lacks even a name at the outset. Moreover, having spent his life with only inanimate objects for friends, he doesn't relate well to actual living creatures. Actor Isla Fisher observes, "He's in his imagination a lot. That's what's interesting about Johnny [Depp] playing him. Johnny would find moments when he's in reality and then in fantasy." Later, Rango lets down his new friends and is humiliated by Rattlesnake Jake, which sends him back to the desert for a spiritual epiphany.

Rango had so many expressions in the storyboards it was nearly impossible to make a rig and model that could do them all. "In a shot where they want him to look mean, they might give him a really strong jaw," says Tim Alexander, who split the job of running ILM's work with John Knoll. (Both have the title of visual effects supervisor.) "Then where they want him to look meek, maybe he doesn't have such a strong jaw." So Rango's controls are complex. Even his teeth are controlled separately.

Lead animator Kevin Martel explains that Rango's tail is an extension of his personality, curled when he's upbeat, dragging when he's tired or depressed. In scenes like his nocturnal return to the desert, "We found if we kept it in a coil, kind of bouncing behind him, it gave him a little too much energy. It had too much life."

As a thespian, Rango uses clothes to help him find the character he's playing, so he has many costume changes, far more than a typical animated character. In fact, the characters in *Rango* change costumes so often the animators took the unusual step of building many costumes separately, with simulated cloth, as opposed to making them part of the character's digital model. That meant the animators had to account for the costume changes. When Rango puts on cowboy boots, for example, he gets taller and walks differently, just as a person would. Even the angles of his hats (he wears five or six) are carefully planned to express his mood. ✪

left: CRASH MᶜCREERY ↯ *Final Fancy Sheriff Color Design*
right: CRASH MᶜCREERY ↯ *Crash on Highway*

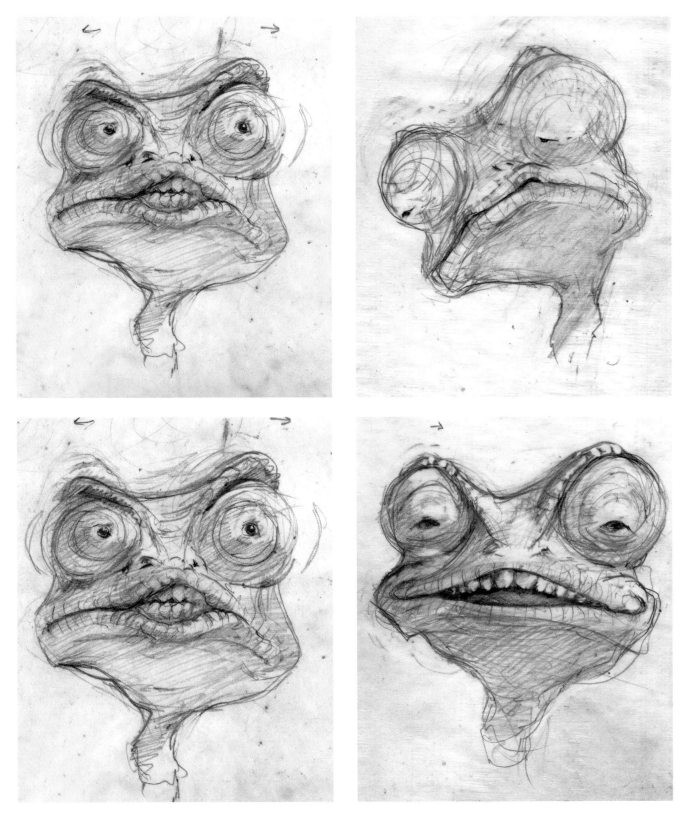

opposite and above: CRASH MᶜCREERY ↵ *Early Rango Expression Tests*

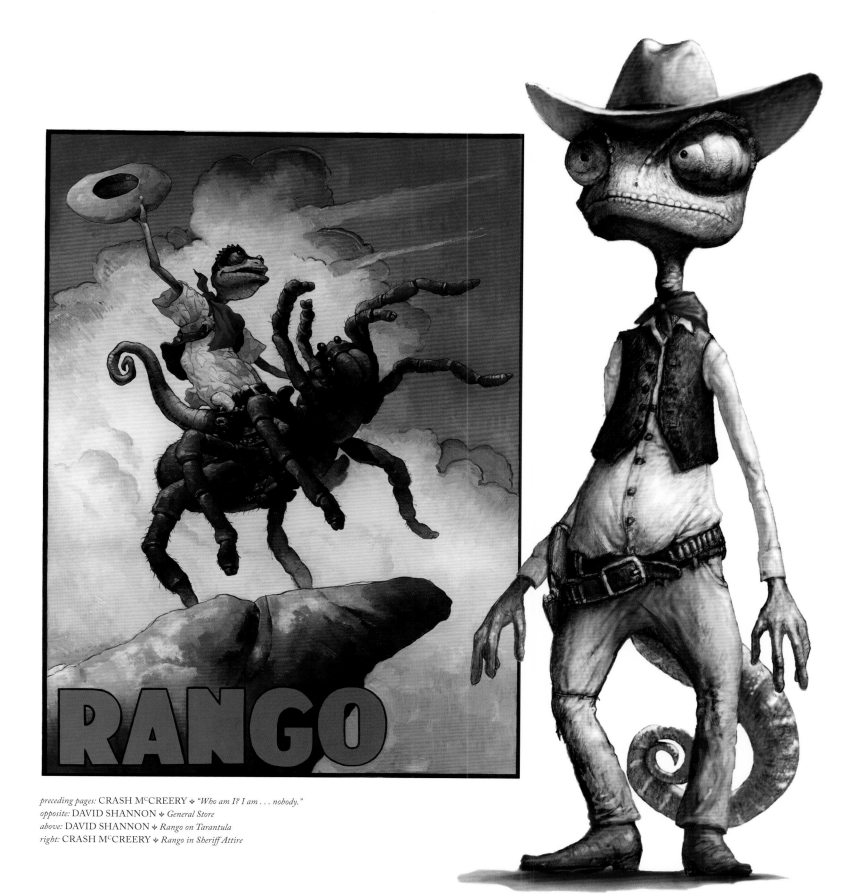

preceding pages: CRASH MᶜCREERY ↯ *"Who am I? I am . . . nobody."*
opposite: DAVID SHANNON ↯ *General Store*
above: DAVID SHANNON ↯ *Rango on Tarantula*
right: CRASH MᶜCREERY ↯ *Rango in Sheriff Attire*

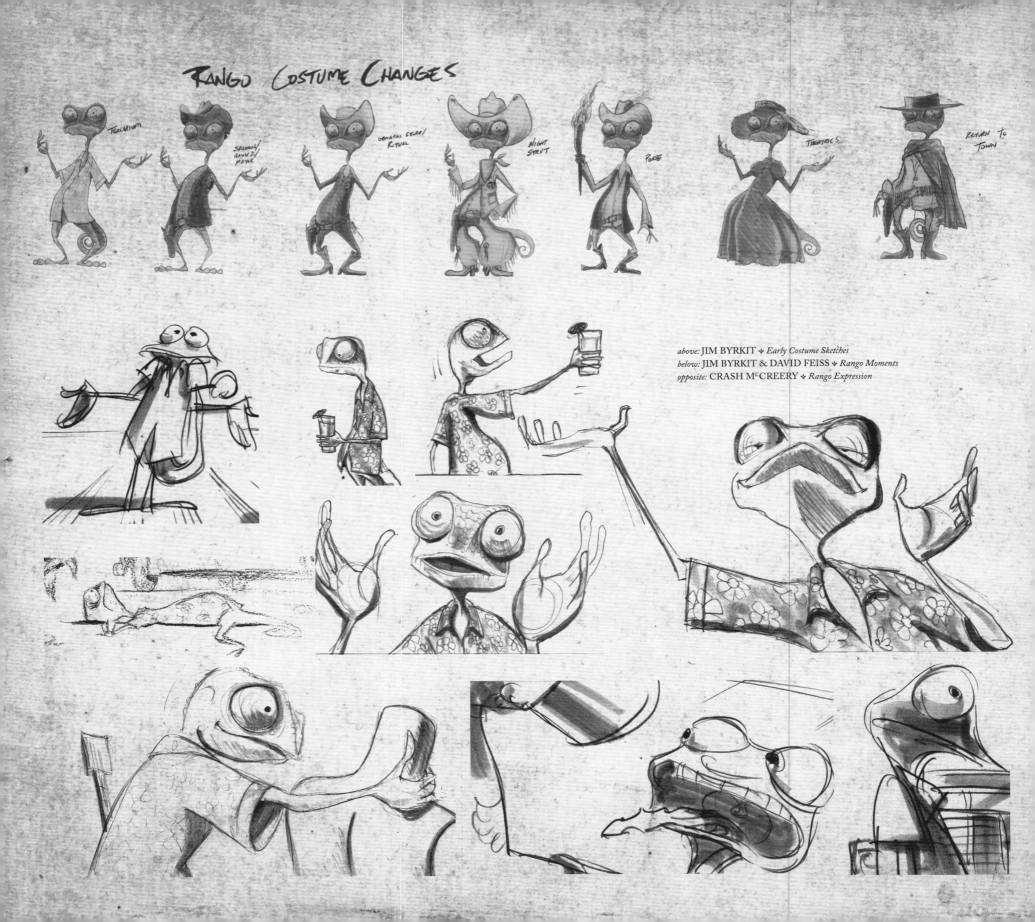

RANGO COSTUME CHANGES

TERRARIUM

SALOON/
HAWK/
MAYOR

GENERAL STORE/
RITUAL

NIGHT
STRUT

POSE

THEATRICS

RETURN TO
TOWN

above: JIM BYRKIT ↓ *Early Costume Sketches*
below: JIM BYRKIT & DAVID FEISS ↓ *Rango Moments*
opposite: CRASH MᶜCREERY ↓ *Rango Expression*

MISS BEANS

✪

PRODUCTION DESIGNER CRASH M^cCREERY SAYS OF RANGO'S SASSY LOVE INTEREST, "SHE'S BEEN ON THE PLAINS, AND SHE'S HAD A HARD LIFE, BUT SHE SURVIVED. SHE'S GOT THAT ACCIDENTALLY attractive kind of feel to her: endearing but tough."

Isla Fisher, who voices Beans, says her character "grew up alone with her father on a ranch and then lost her father. All she has is the land. She's sort of her own little island. She doesn't have friends. She's not a particularly socialized lizard, so to speak."

Beans's lead animator, Maia Kayser, observes, "[Beans] carries a lot of baggage, a lot of issues about her dad. But she does come off very confident. She wears this hard shell at the beginning, although she wears her heart on her sleeve. She'll just blurt out things every now and then."

Beans actually proved as hard to write as she was to design. "All the other characters are so extreme and so funny, including Rango, and she was too much of a straight woman," says writer John Logan. "She wasn't funny enough." Logan, the old movie buff, gave her a dash of Katharine Hepburn's fire and a little Jean Arthur, too. "If I had Bob Hope and Jean Arthur, I could do *Rango*," he says.

Holly Hunter was a main inspiration for Fisher. She laughs, "I know all of Holly Hunter's lines from any movie she's ever done." She also threw in a bit of Clint Eastwood's growl. "It just gave her more of a gravelly, slower pace."

Producer John Carls says, "Isla certainly brings the heart and soul of that character to life, so that helps a lot. She did a beautiful performance." Beans acquired red hair from Fisher, too.

Matching the looks of Beans and Rango was difficult. Rango's head was so large at times it looked like he could swallow her whole. He has small eyes and a big mouth, while she has big eyes and a small mouth. In the end, McCreery says, "I'm really happy with the way she came out, and the way Isla's voice matches what's on screen. I feel like that was a great marriage between the visual and what she brought voice-wise." ✪

left : JIM BYRKIT ↓ *Beans, Stump, and Bill*
right: JIM BYRKIT ↓ *Beans Ritual Sketch*
opposite: CRASH M^cCREERY ↓ *Beans's Head*

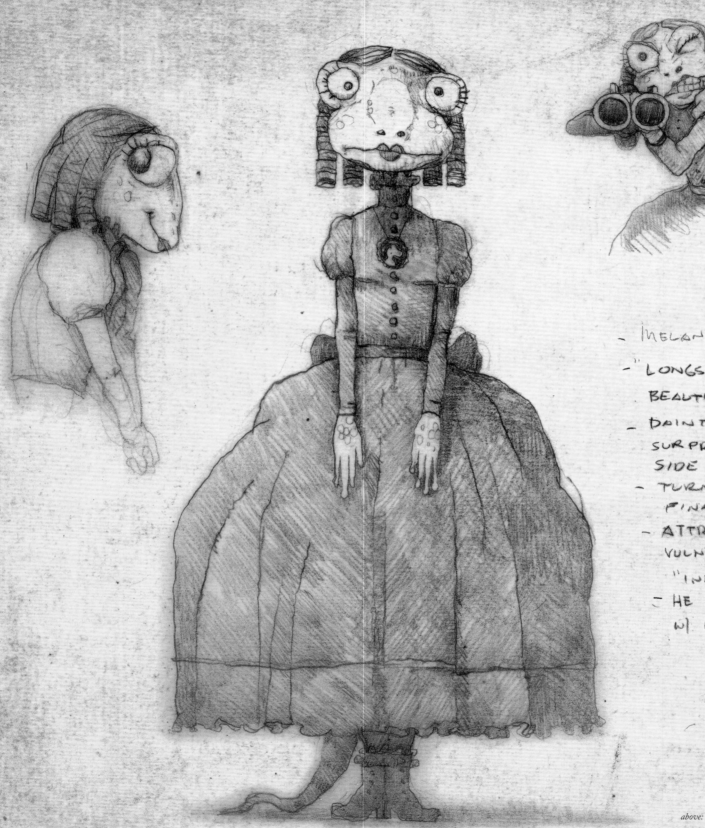

- MELANCHOLY, POETIC, SHY
- "LONGS FOR/WAXES ABOUT
  BEAUTY & WATER
- DAINTINESS HIDES A
  SURPRISING TOUGH-AS-NAILS
  SIDE
- TURNS THE TIDE IN
  FINAL SHOWDOWN?,
- ATTRACTED TO RANGO'S
  VULNERABILITY? HIS
  "INNER BEAUTY"
- HE MAKES HER LAUGH
  W/ HIS CHARACTERIZATIONS

above: DAVID SHANNON ✤ *Beans Original Hero Sketches*

above: CRASH McCREERY ❧ *Beans in Color*
right: ILM ❧ *Final Render*

THE MARIACHI OWLS

⭐

DIRECTOR GORE VERBINSKI AND HEAD OF STORY JIM BYRKIT WERE PONDERING THE IDEA OF A MEXICAN GREEK CHORUS TO FOLLOW RANGO AROUND WHEN PRODUCTION DESIGNER CRASH McCREERY HANDED THEM a sketch of a mariachi of owls. The idea clicked, and the Mariachi Owls became *Rango*'s pessimistic narrators.

Maia Kayser, the lead animator for Beans, asked to lead the Mariachi Owls as well. "The accordion [player, Señor Flan] is the main narrator," she says. "He's pretty much the leader of the band. He doesn't show much emotion. The violinist [Lupe], he's more in his own world, and he's always happy when he's doing his music.

"I tended to play the trumpet guy [Chico] kind of jolly but always playing along with the performance that was needed at that moment. In one shot, for example, we had the trumpet guy hanging from a noose, kind of playing dead, then playing his trumpet a little bit and flopping down again. So he's always playing along. The guitarist [Raoul] is usually joining in on the whole . . . They're kind of into performance. That's what they do. They perform." ✪

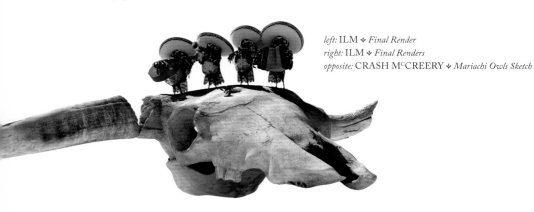

left: ILM ↓ *Final Render*
right: ILM ↓ *Final Renders*
opposite: CRASH McCREERY ↓ *Mariachi Owls Sketch*

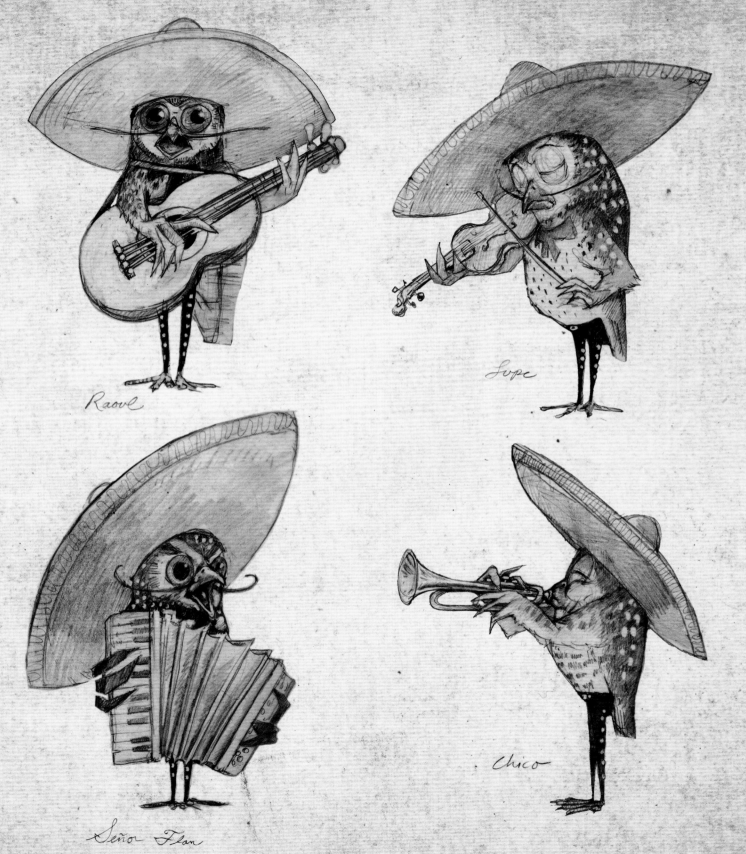

Raoul

Lope

Señor Flan

Chico

PRISCILLA

★

"**SHE'S VERY MUCH A LITTLE GOTH GIRL,**" SAYS ACTOR ABIGAIL BRESLIN. "**IF SHE WAS A REAL-LIFE TEENAGER, SHE'D HAVE BLACK NAILS. SHE'S VERY HONEST. SHE'S VERY MORBID. SHE'S NOT UNHAPPY;** she's just telling people she knows they're going to die, and she's sorry about that, but what can she profit off of it?" Breslin adds, "She's really cute, but don't tell her I said that, because she won't like that."

Priscilla began as an off-kilter take on Brandon De Wilde in *Shane*, the boy who comes to idolize the gunfighter, with a bit of Kim Darby in *True Grit* mixed in. Her look is based on the aye-aye lemur of Madagascar, which isn't a desert creature, but once production designer Crash McCreery saw a photo of one, it didn't matter. "It had these big eyes and the little pointy mouth. I was like, 'Oh, my god, we've got to use that.'"

If Priscilla is Goth, her playmates are downright rough. Dutch is a mean punk, Cletus is clueless, and Lucky is missing an eye and a finger from playing with fireworks. His suppurating eye patch is testament to life's being hard in Dirt. ☻

left: JIM BYRKIT ❧ *Priscilla Armed*
above: EUGENE YELCHIN ❧ *Orphan Priscilla*

above: CRASH M^CCREERY ✦ *Final Priscilla*
right: ILM ✦ *Early Model after Render*

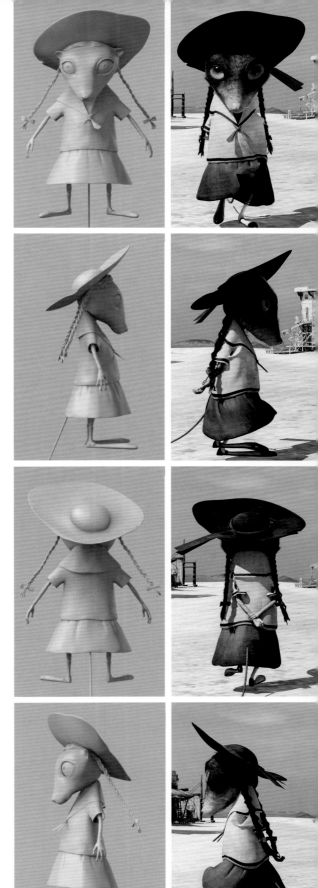

left: CRASH M^CCREERY ↓ *Final Mayor Design*
above: DAVID SHANNON ↓ *Early Mayor Sketch*
opposite, top: CRASH M^CCREERY ↓ *Mayor Terrarium*
opposite, bottom: CRASH M^CCREERY ↓ *"Water, Mr. Rango."*

THE MAYOR

⭐

"I LOVE THE MAYOR," SAYS ACTOR NED BEATTY. FIRST, BEATTY JUST LIKES TURTLES. SECOND, HE DOESN'T SEE THE MAYOR AS EVIL, EXACTLY, JUST AS SOMEONE WHO UNDERSTANDS WHAT IT TAKES TO build the future. "I'm not sure he would be judgmental about right and wrong," says Beatty. "I think where he's coming from is that this is the way it's done. If some of the people suffer some of the time, that's just too bad, because this is the way it must be done. We must preserve the water."

Director Gore Verbinksi echoes this idea that the Mayor is not evil per se, but is rather more like a representation of progress, which is so often indifferent. "Progress is a force, an inevitability like death," he says. "It is coming. The Mayor simply represents the end of an era—the era of heroes."

The Mayor is unabashedly based on John Huston's malevolent Noah Cross in *Chinatown*. As it happens, Beatty was directed by Huston in two films and remembers him well. "He was 'Mr. Huston,' and he was also 'Yes, sir. No, sir.' He was quite a presence." Beatty does Huston's voice dead-on.

Putting the Mayor in a wheelchair added to his menace. Production designer Crash McCreery says, "I'm wondering if this comes from biblical stories, where when the devil fell to Earth, he hit so hard that he broke his leg or something like that. So whenever you see classic depictions of the devil, he's got a cane. There's this kind of false sense of security that you get from seeing [a character] in a wheelchair, that they're not as dangerous. Their evil doesn't come from them being physically intimidating. Their evil is deeper than that." ✪

RATTLESNAKE JAKE

★

ACTOR BILL NIGHY CALLS RATTLESNAKE JAKE "VIOLENTLY HORRIBLE" AND SAYS, "I TRIED TO MAKE HIM THAT GUY THEY GET FROM OUT OF TOWN, THE FIERCEST, BADDEST GUY THEY BRING IN TO TAKE care of business ... So my job therefore is to be as scary as possible, though there is, if you'll forgive the pun, a twist in the tale."

Production designer Crash McCreery based Jake's design on classic Western heavy Lee Van Cleef. "For me, [Jake] encapsulates everything that's scary about a villain. We talked about him being albino at one point, just because he's death, basically. But I'm really glad we stuck with the classic rattlesnake, because people are terrified of rattlesnakes anyway. I think he's one of the most successful characters in the film. Kids are going to pee in their pants when they see him." By design, Jake's bulk almost always spills out of frame. Only at the climax, when he's vulnerable, is all of Jake seen in a frame.

Snakes are always a problem in computer animation, and Rattlesnake Jake was even more so. "He's been kind of hell to work with," says lead animator Jakub Pistecky. "He has a lot of controllers, and most animators, when they opened him up and looked at his interface, gasped a little bit. [His rig] is deceivingly tricky to work with, which kind of fits with his personality." ✪

opposite: CRASH M^cCREERY ↘ *Final Jake Color Design*
top: EUGENE YELCHIN ↘ *Early Jake Sketch*
left: CRASH M^cCREERY ↘ *Early Jake Design*
above: EUGENE YELCHIN ↘ *Jake Tail Concept*
following pages: CRASH M^cCREERY ↘ *"Where do you think I come from?"*

IN THE SNAKE'S SKIN

WITH HIS DARK STUBBLE, intense gaze, and burly arms, Jakub "Jake the Snake" Pistecky looks like a man you'd want on your side in a bar fight. It's not hard to see why he was chosen to lead *Rango*'s villains. Visual effects supervisor John Knoll calls the choice "brilliant casting on [animation supervisor] Hal [Hickel]'s part." Everyone swears Jakub's nickname is just a coincidence.

Pistecky is a Czech-born Canadian who studied in Vancouver, and his résumé at ILM includes animating Yoda in the recent *Star Wars* films and work on two of the *Harry Potter* pictures. For the fourth film in that series, Pistecky animated another prominent reptile, the Hungarian Horntail dragon.

"I kind of connect with Jake," says Pistecky. "He's the . . . outsider, very passionate about what he does. I had a strong admiration for him, not only in terms of the rattlesnake as a lone gunman but [also because of] the connection between him and Lee Van Cleef in the *Dollars* trilogy. [Cleef] always [played] my favorite characters . . . " ⊛

left: CRASH M^cCREERY ⋇ *Jake Eye*
above: JIM BYRKIT ⋇ *Jake Shootout Storyboard*

above: CRASH M^CCREERY ⌄ *Roadkill Final Hole*
opposite, left: ILM ⌄ *Final Renders*
opposite, right: DAVID SHANNON ⌄ *Early Roadkill Sketch*
following pages: CRASH M^CCREERY ⌄ *"You are a very lonley lizard."*

ROADKILL

★

"**R**OADKILL BECAME OUR VERSION OF CARLOS CASTANEDA MIXED WITH A BOTTLE OF BOURBON AND DON QUIXOTE," SAYS WRITER JOHN LOGAN OF RANGO'S SPIRITUAL GUIDE. DIRECTOR GORE VERBINSKI told actor Alfred Molina, who did Roadkill's voice, to think of him as a border-town mystic. "I think Gore's description was absolutely on the money," says Molina. "He's talking about getting to the other side of the road, but it's all metaphor. He's a very mysterious character." Molina's secret inspiration for the voice was Anthony Quinn, who played a spiritual guide of sorts in *Zorba the Greek*.

Shawn Kelly, lead animator for Roadkill, says his team at first made him a kindly Obi-Wan Kenobi character. But Verbinski told them, "'He is wise and he is friendly, but he's also a seeker,'" Kelly says. "[Verbinski] wanted crazy eyes. I think once we got just a little hint of insanity in there, then [Roadkill] really came together." ✪

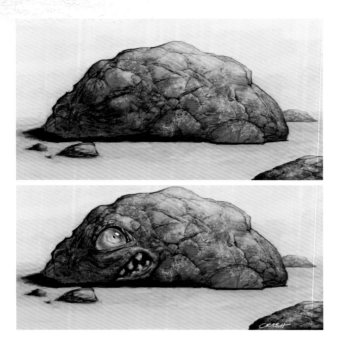

ROCK EYE

★

WRITER JOHN LOGAN CALLS ROCK EYE "VITALLY IMPORTANT." BECAUSE RANGO'S FIRST INTERACTIONS AFTER LEAVING HIS TERRARIUM "SET THE THEMATIC POINT OF THE MOVIE." Roadkill sends Rango on his quest, then Rock Eye teaches him the importance of "blending in."

Rock Eye was difficult to design and animate because he had to actually look like a rock, with no visible seams. "He doesn't make a lot of sense, really," says production designer Crash McCreery. "He's a frog living in the desert. It kind of felt right. We just went with it. A frog seemed funny, and that kind of image fit the character." ✪

above: CRASH MᶜCREERY ↓ *Hero Rock Eye Progression*
right: JIM BYRKIT ↓ *Rock Eye Expression Tests*
opposite: CRASH MᶜCREERY ↓ *Final Rock Eye Color Design*

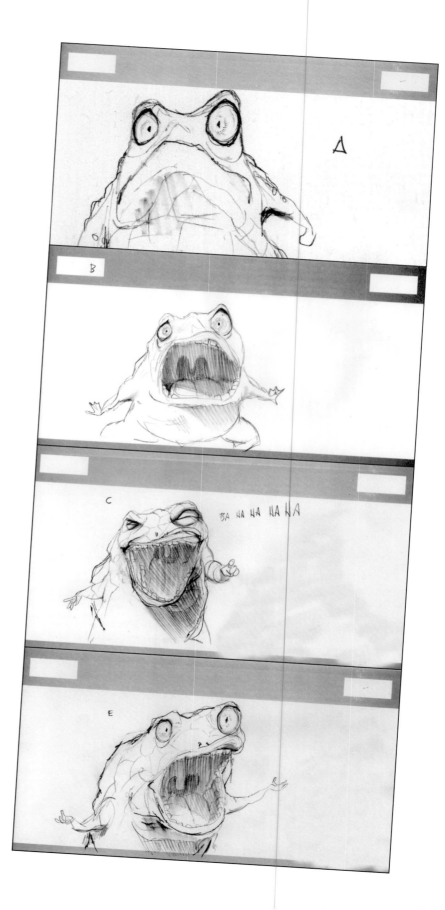

top: CRASH M^CCREERY ⬎ *Hawk Top View*
right: CRASH M^CCREERY ⬎ *Original Hawk Concept*

THE HAWK

★

"**S**OMETIMES, IN A WORLD OF PERSONALITIES," SAYS DIRECTOR GORE VERBINSKI, "THE CONTRAST OF SOMETHING DEVOID OF CHARISMA–A COLD REALISTIC KILLING MACHINE–HAS MORE impact. The nameless 'hawk.'"

"His beak is cracked, and the tip has been replaced with a silver filigreed tip like you'd find on the toe of a cowboy boot," says animation supervisor Hal Hickel. "But outside of that, he's just a red-tailed hawk. He's mean. He doesn't talk."

Birds are difficult to animate because it's hard to make their wings fold up properly, and their feathers are very complex. Yet a biologist told Hickel she was impressed by this hawk's realism. "I took that as high praise 'cause she's very picky about those things," he says. ☉

left: ILM ↡ *Final Renders*
top: CRASH M^cCREERY ↡ *Early Hawk Sketches*
above: CRASH M^cCREERY ↡ *Early Hawk Scene Concept*

CACTUS SPIRITS

✪

"**T**HEY HAD TO BE KIND OF IMPOSING AND MAGICAL," SAYS LEAD ANIMATOR SHAWN KELLY, YET ON THE OTHER HAND, "[DIRECTOR] GORE VERBINSKI WANTED THEM TO REALLY FEEL LIKE THEY were on their last legs. They need some water really bad. And giving them personality was another challenge. How do you give this tubular plant a personality?"

The legend that the Cactus Spirits can move proves true, but making them move was a thorny problem. "You have this huge network of roots tearing out of the ground and ripping free and digging back in and pulling," says Kelly. "It's a lot of different little pieces to keep track of. Two or three of the animators mostly did the cactus work. They really jumped on the grenade and battled through some tough stuff but made it really cool." ✪

left: JURGEN GROSS ↓ *Original Cactus Spirit*
above: AARON MᶜBRIDE ↓ *Cactus Spirit Concept*
opposite, top: CRASH MᶜCREERY ↓ *Dream Spirit 1*
opposite, bottom: CRASH MᶜCREERY ↓ *Dream Spirit 3*

THE POSSE

◆─────★─────◆

THE MEMBERS OF THE POSSE MOUNT THEIR ROADRUNNERS TO RIDE WITH SHERIFF RANGO AFTER DIRT'S STOLEN WATER. THEY GET A LOT OF SCREEN TIME, SO THEY HAD TO BE very distinct. Verbinski wanted a dysfunctional posse like the group of inmates in *One Flew Over the Cuckoo's Nest*—distinct characters that complement each another. "One's optimistic, the Doc is always drunk, and [Wounded Bird] is knowledgeable but silent," says production designer Crash McCreery. "So we had this classic kind of collection of characters that all played off of each other really well."

To accentuate each character's personality, the artists spent a lot of time refining their appearances. Continues McCreery: "We paid laborious attention to their details, their clothing. I drove ILM crazy by saying, 'Oh, the nose is a little too small' or 'Can you bring that hair down over the eye just a little bit more?' It's amazing how detail can really change the appearance of a character."

Art director Aaron McBride notes, "We give them sort of bloodshot eyes with fat deposits in the whites so they feel like they've been squinting in a sandstorm for forty years and are not all quite right in the head." That's especially true of Sgt. Turley, a clumsy veteran who is unaware of the arrow through his eye and skull. He complains of trouble in the *other* eye: "That there is conjunctivitis, sir. It's hereditary." Turley is voiced by director Gore Verbinski, who also voices a half dozen townsfolk and desert rodents. ✪

right: JOHN BELL, CHRISTIAN ALZMANN & CRASH M^cCREERY ♥ *Posse Search*

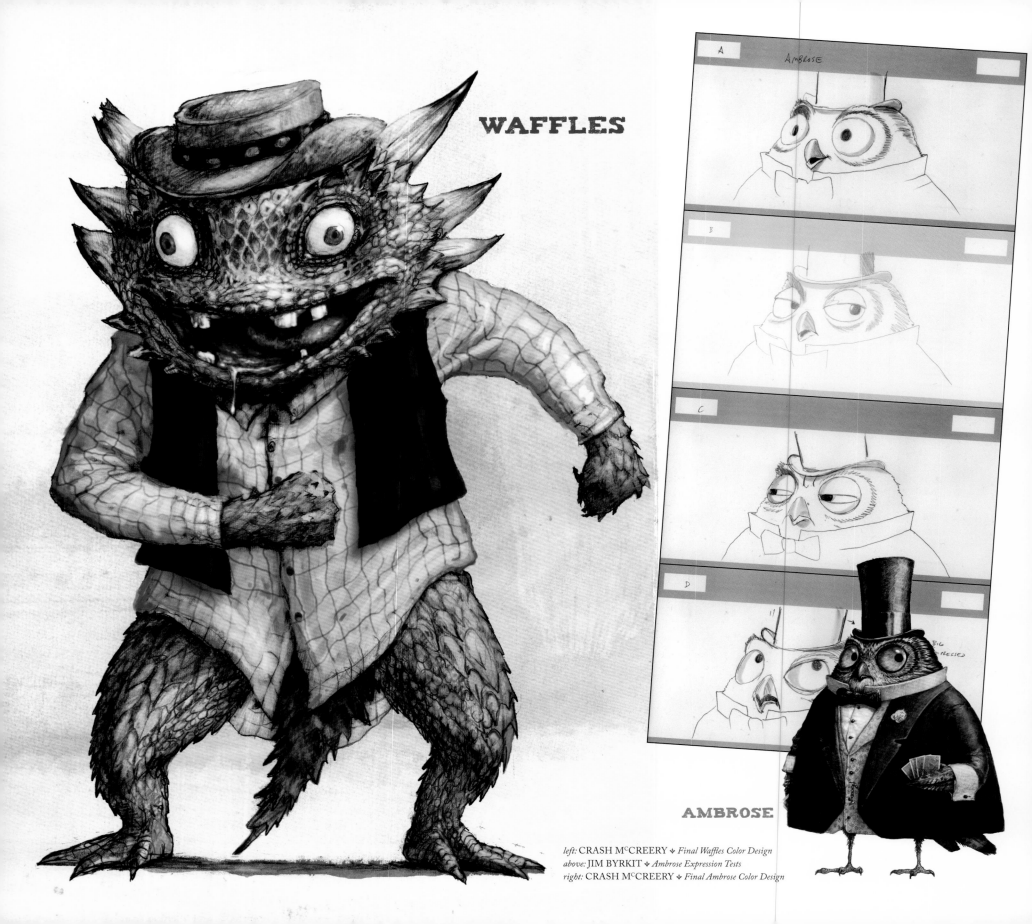

WAFFLES

AMBROSE

A AMBROSE

B

C

D

left: CRASH M^CCREERY ↓ *Final Waffles Color Design*
above: JIM BYRKIT ↓ *Ambrose Expression Tests*
right: CRASH M^CCREERY ↓ *Final Ambrose Color Design*

DOC

BUFORD

BARTENDER (TOAD)

ROADRUNNERS

SGT. TURLEY

clockwise from top left: CRASH MᶜCREERY ⤸ *Final Doc Color Design;* CRASH MᶜCREERY ⤸ *Final Buford Color Design;* CRASH MᶜCREERY ⤸ *Buford Concept;* CRASH MᶜCREERY ⤸ *Final Sgt. Turley Color Design;* EUGENE YELCHIN ⤸ *Early Buford Sketch;* CRASH MᶜCREERY ⤸ *Final Roadrunner Color Design*

ELGIN

WOUNDED
BIRD

MR. FURGUS

far left: CRASH M^cCREERY ⚘ *Final Elgin Color Design*
left: CRASH M^cCREERY ⚘ *Furgus Concept*
above: CRASH M^cCREERY ⚘ *Wounded Bird Concept*

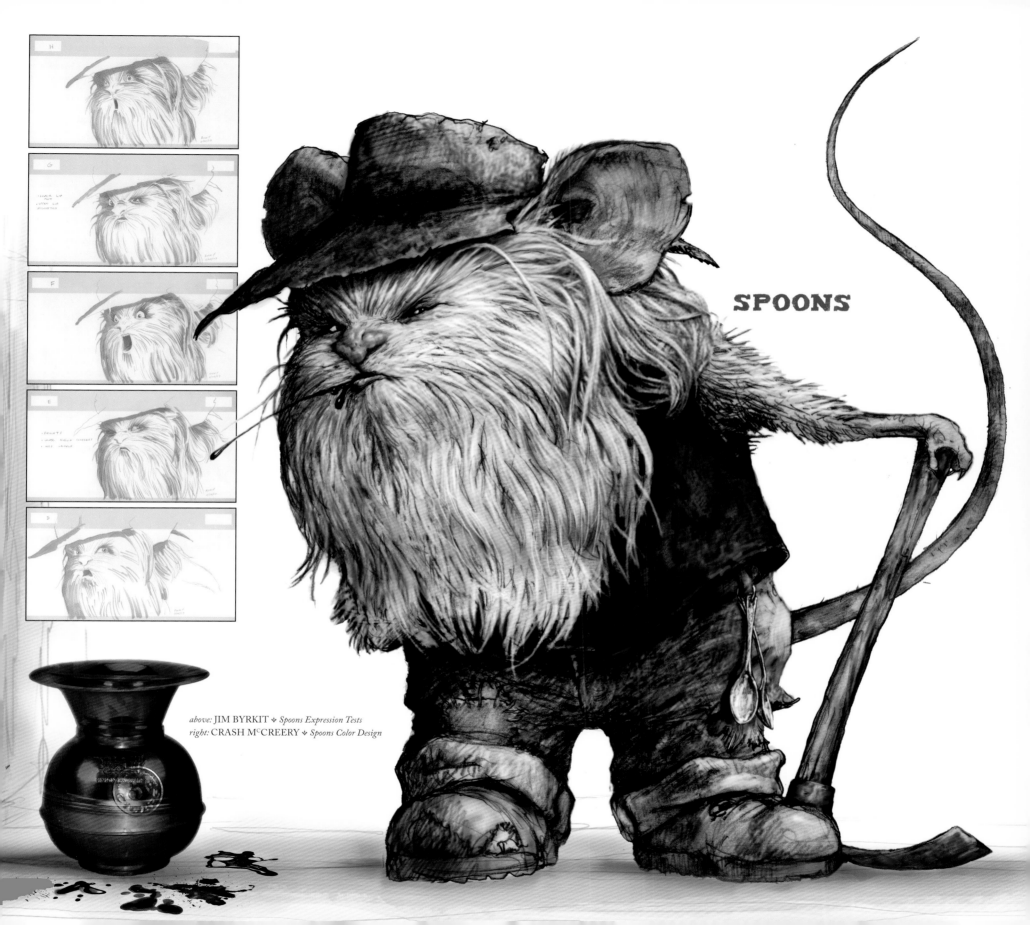

SPOONS

above: JIM BYRKIT ✧ *Spoons Expression Tests*
right: CRASH M^CCREERY ✧ *Spoons Color Design*

BAD BILL
& HIS GANG

"**A**N OUT-AND-OUT BULLY," SAYS ACTOR RAY WINSTONE OF BAD BILL. "HE'S LIKE SOME OF THE OLD GUNSLINGERS YOU SEE IN THE MOVIES. THEY'RE FINE AS LONG AS THEY'VE GOT LITTLE GUYS in front of them—until they meet the big guy that comes to town. When he sees there's no fear in someone's eyes, he has the fear in *his* eyes."

Lead animator Jakub Pistecky says, "[Bad Bill] is mean and cocky at the same time, and I think that just plays power-fully on the screen." Producer David Shannon originally imag-ined a bowler-hatted Gila monster, and the idea stuck. Bill's cockney accent is inspired by producer Graham King.

Bill's henchmen are Kinski, Chorizo, and Stump. Kinski's look and personality are influenced by a hunchback Klaus Kinski played in spaghetti Westerns. "He's a little bit more psychotic," says Pistecky. "The other two are more goofballs. They're kind of the dumb boys of the operation." ✪

right: CRASH McCREERY ↓ *Final Bad Bill Color Design*

left: DAVID SHANNON ↳ *Original Bad Bill Concept*
above: CRASH M^cCREERY ↳ *Bad Bill Scared*

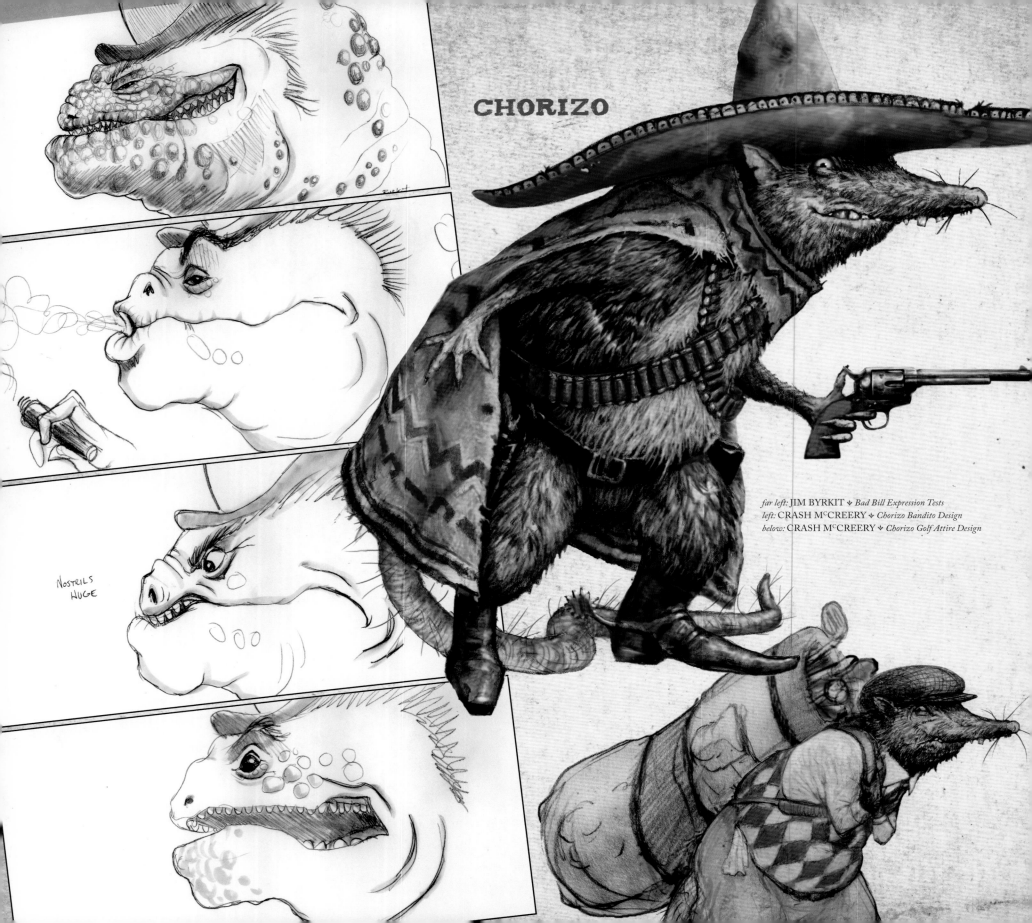

CHORIZO

far left: JIM BYRKIT ↳ *Bad Bill Expression Tests*
left: CRASH MᶜCREERY ↳ *Chorizo Bandito Design*
below: CRASH MᶜCREERY ↳ *Chorizo Golf Attire Design*

NOSTRILS HUGE

STUMP

KINSKI

top left: CRASH MᶜCREERY ↓ *Stump Color Design*
left: CRASH MᶜCREERY ↓ *Original Kinski Concept*
above: CRASH MᶜCREERY ↓ *Kinski Color Design*
right: CRASH MᶜCREERY ↓ *Kinski Sketch*

DENIZENS
OF DIRT

---✦---

MODEL SUPERVISOR GEOFF CAMPBELL PEGS ONE FEELING THE CHARACTERS' FACES HAD IN COMMON: THEY SEEMED STRESSED AND DESPERATE. "I WANTED TO MAKE SURE WE WERE PUTTING some of that into these models even before animation," says Campbell. "If the brow shows a lot of years, if it's someone aged before their time. We were trying to build some of that in so you'd see some of the angst on their faces, and even at rest you'd get a sense of that tension. And on top of that, [director] Gore [Verbinski] really wanted to make sure nothing was symmetrical, so we'd have to beat them up quite a bit. Sometimes you'd really lopside a face. A lot of them have wounds and things like that."

They sweat a lot, too, like spaghetti Western characters perspiring from tension. Even lizards, who in real life don't have sweat glands, glisten with sweat in *Rango*. ✦

right: ILM ✦ *Saloon Crowd Final Render*

MELONEE

BARON VON HOOSENSCHITZEL

above: CRASH McCREERY ↴ *Final Baron Von Hoosenschitzel Color Design*
below: CRASH McCREERY ↴ *Final Hazel Moats Color Design*

HAZEL MOATS

top: EUGENE YELCHIN ↴ *Melonee Concept*
above: CRASH McCREERY ↴ *Final Melonee Color Design*

CRISPIN

FRESCA

above: CRASH M^CCREERY ⬇ *Final Crispin Color Design*
top right: EUGENE YELCHIN ⬇ *Original Crispin Concept*
above right: CRASH M^CCREERY ⬇ *Crispin Sketch*
below: CRASH M^CCREERY ⬇ *Final Anvil Color Design*

above left: EUGENE YELCHIN ⬇ *Original Fresca Sketch*
above right: CRASH M^CCREERY ⬇ *Fresca Concept*
right: CRASH M^CCREERY ⬇ *Final Fresca Color Design*
below: CRASH M^CCREERY ⬇ *Final Javelina Color Design*

ANVIL

JAVELINA

MR. BLACK

GORDY

CLINKER

left: CRASH MᶜCREERY ⚓ *Final Gordy Color Design*
top: CRASH MᶜCREERY ⚓ *Final Mr. Black Color Design*
right: CRASH MᶜCREERY ⚓ *Final Clinker Color Design*

HITCH

R.I.P.

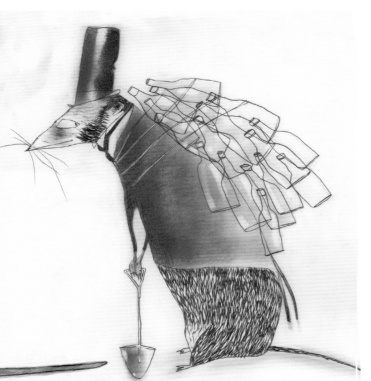

CURLY

top left: CRASH MᶜCREERY ↓ *R.I.P. Sketch*
top: CRASH MᶜCREERY ↓ *Hitch Color Design*
left: EUGENE YELCHIN ↓ *Original Clinker Concept*
right: CRASH MᶜCREERY ↓ *Final Curly Color Design*

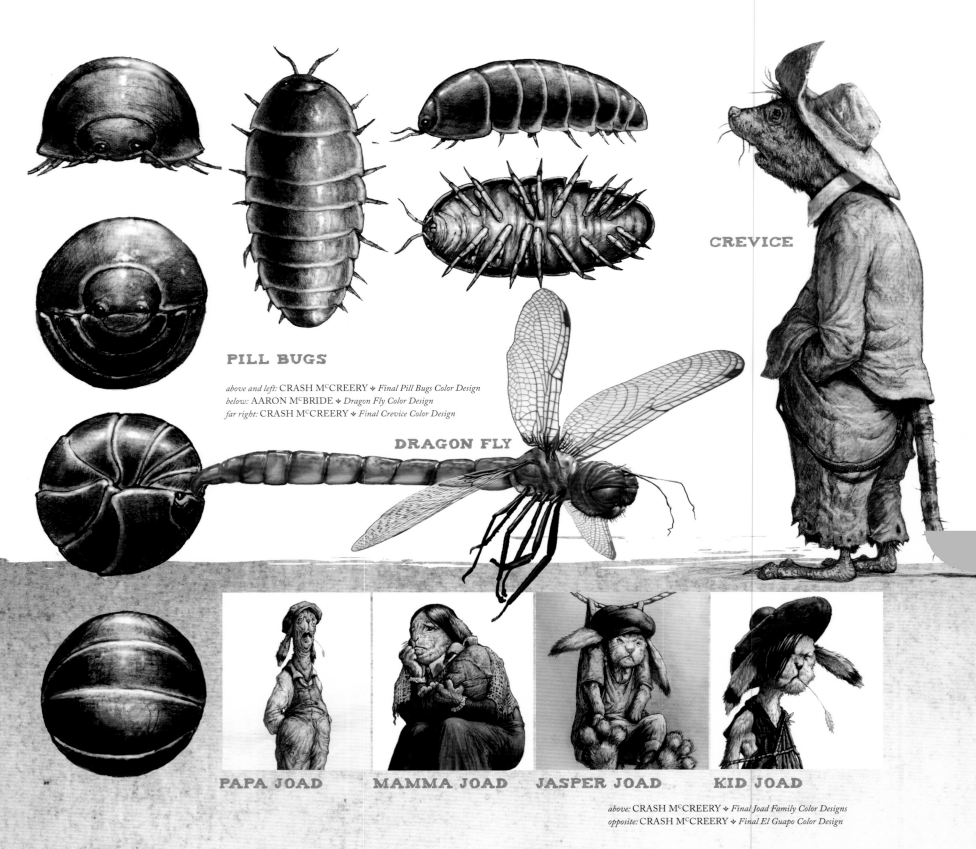

PILL BUGS

above and left: CRASH M^CCREERY ↯ *Final Pill Bugs Color Design*
below: AARON M^CBRIDE ↯ *Dragon Fly Color Design*
far right: CRASH M^CCREERY ↯ *Final Crevice Color Design*

CREVICE

DRAGON FLY

PAPA JOAD

MAMMA JOAD

JASPER JOAD

KID JOAD

above: CRASH M^CCREERY ↯ *Final Joad Family Color Designs*
opposite: CRASH M^CCREERY ↯ *Final El Guapo Color Design*

EL GUAPO

ANGELIQUE

clockwise from top left: CRASH MᶜCREERY ✤ *Final Angelique Color Design;* EUGENE YELCHIN ✤ *Original Angelique Concept;* ANTHONY LEONARDI III ✤ *Angelique Orthos;* AARON MᶜBRIDE & CRASH MᶜCREERY ✤ *Bar Fly Color Designs;* CRASH MᶜCREERY ✤ *Final Cletus Color Design;* CRASH MᶜCREERY ✤ *Final Lenny Color Design*

BAR FLY

LENNY

CLETUS

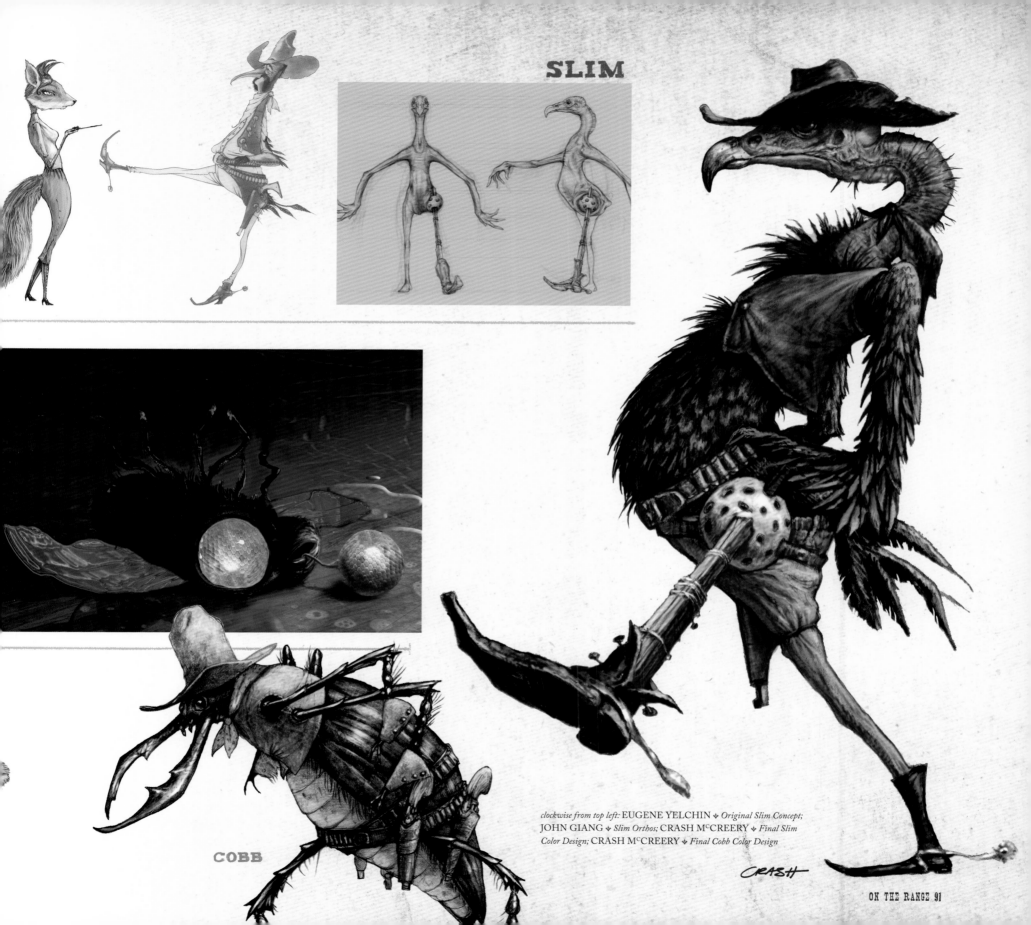

SLIM

clockwise from top left: EUGENE YELCHIN ↳ *Original Slim Concept;*
JOHN GIANG ↳ *Slim Orthos;* CRASH M^cCREERY ↳ *Final Slim
Color Design;* CRASH M^cCREERY ↳ *Final Cobb Color Design*

COBB

CRASH

DELILAH

LUCKY

left: CRASH M^CCREERY ↴ *Final Delilah Color Design*
above: CRASH M^CCREERY ↴ *Final Lucky Color Design*

SALOON

ELBOWS

above: JIM BYRKIT ↴ *Original Elbows Sketch*
right: CRASH M^CCREERY ↴ *Final Elbows Color Design*

MISS DAISY

BONNIE

DUTCH

BOO

PARSONS

left: CRASH M^cCREERY ↳ *Final Parsons Color Design*
below: CRASH M^cCREERY ↳ *Parsons Concept*

left: CRASH M^cCREERY ↳ *Final Miss Daisy Color Design*
top: ANTHONY LEONARDI III ↳ *Bonnie Orthos*
above: EUGENE YELCHIN ↳ *Original Bonnie Sketch*
right: CRASH M^cCREERY ↳ *Final Bonnie Color Design*
below left: CRASH M^cCREERY ↳ *Final Boo Color Design*
below: CRASH M^cCREERY ↳ *Final Dutch Color Design*

JEREMIAH

MORDECAI

SOD BUSTER

left: CRASH M^CCREERY ☙ *Final Jeremiah Color Design*
top: CRASH M^CCREERY ☙ *Final Mordecai Color Design*
above: CRASH M^CCREERY ☙ *Final Sod Buster Color Design*

MR. MERRIMACK

MR.
SNUGGLES

ACOLYTES

top: CRASH MᶜCREERY ↓ *Final Mr. Merrimack Color Design*
above: CRASH MᶜCREERY ↓ *Final Acolyte Color Design*
right: CRASH MᶜCREERY ↓ *Original Mr. Snuggles Concept*
far right: CRASH MᶜCREERY ↓ *Final Mr. Snuggles Color Design*

BALTHAZAR
& THE INBRED RODENTS

"**O**NE OF THE MOST ENTERTAINING THINGS ABOUT WORKING ON THIS IS YOU GET TO WRITE THE MOST EXTREME CHARACTERS YOU COULD POSSIBLY IMAGINE, AND THEN YOU GET TO MAKE THEM MORE extreme," says writer John Logan. The Inbred Rodents are a good example. "[Director] Gore [Verbinski], [head of story] Jim [Byrkit], and I all love Flannery O'Connor, and we loved *Wise Blood*. So from that came the blind Balthazar, like an Old Testament preacher who sort of hustles and connives his way through life."

Balthazar is accompanied by two brothers: smaller, smarter Ezekiel and oafish Jedidiah. Jedidiah's hand gestures were inspired by actor Ryan Hurst's performance on the live recording stage; a careful look at them reveals he's not exactly dumb, he just needs time to work things out.

Generally, the Rodents are a clan of pariahs, and Verbinski wanted them creepy. "They were not comfortably evolved," says art director Aaron McBride. "They're sort of accidental life-forms." Animation supervisor Hal Hickel calls their big scene "a little bit *The Hills Have Eyes* meets *Deliverance*." ◉

right: CRASH M^cCREERY ↓ *Final Balthazar Color Design*

EZEKIEL

JEDIDIAH

BATS

top left: CRASH MᶜCREERY ↳ Final Ezekiel Color Design
left: CRASH MᶜCREERY ↳ Final Jedidiah Color Design
above: EUGENE YELCHIN ↳ Original Bats Concept
right and far right: CRASH MᶜCREERY ↳ Final Bats Designs

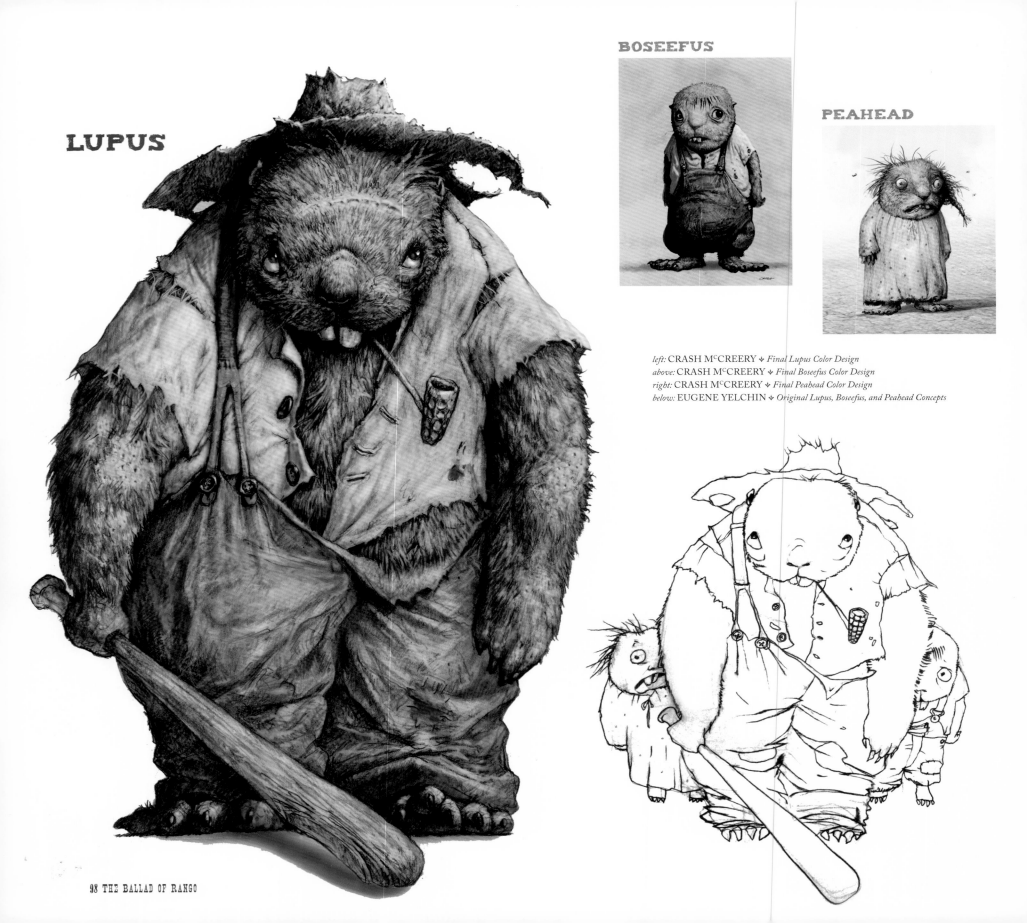

LUPUS

BOSEEFUS

PEAHEAD

left: CRASH M^CCREERY ↘ *Final Lupus Color Design*
above: CRASH M^CCREERY ↘ *Final Boseefus Color Design*
right: CRASH M^CCREERY ↘ *Final Peahead Color Design*
below: EUGENE YELCHIN ↘ *Original Lupus, Boseefus, and Peahead Concepts*

MAYBELLE

BUCKET LADY

top: CRASH MᶜCREERY ꙮ *Final Maybelle Color Design*
above left: EUGENE YELCHIN ꙮ *Original Bucket Lady Concept*
above right: CRASH MᶜCREERY ꙮ *Final Bucket Lady Color Design*
right: CRASH MᶜCREERY ꙮ *Original Granny Concept*

GRANNY

STOOLS

COWBOY RODENT

LASSO
RODENT

GRUMPER

opposite, far left: CRASH MᶜCREERY ↳ *Final Lasso Rodent Design*
opposite, top right: JOHN GIANG & AARON MᶜBRIDE ↳ *Final Stools Color Design*
opposite, middle right: EUGENE YELCHIN ↳ *Stools Sketch*
opposite, bottom right: JOHN GIANG ↳ *Final Cowboy Rodent Color Design*
top: AARON MᶜBRIDE ↳ *Final Grumper Color Design*
above: EUGENE YELCHIN ↳ *Original Grumper Concept*
right: CRASH MᶜCREERY ↳ *Final Banjo Rat Color Design*

BANJO RAT

COUSIN MURT

KNIFE ATTACKER RODENT

SPURTS

SALOON

above: CRASH MᶜCREERY ↴ *Final Cousin Murt Color Design*
top right: CRASH MᶜCREERY ↴ *Cousin Murt Sketch*
top far right: CARLOS HUANTE & CRASH MᶜCREERY ↴ *Final Knife Attacker Rodent Design*
right: AARON MᶜBRIDE ↴ *Final Spurts Color Design*

A PAIN IN THE EYES

"IT'S THE THINGS you don't think are going to be a pain in the ass that actually are the pain in the ass," says animation supervisor Hal Hickel. One example: the case of the refractive eyes.

ILM decided, somewhat ambitiously as it turned out, to give their animal characters anatomically correct eyes. Unlike humans, some animals have their pupils near the center of the orb, so when the eye rotates, the pupils barely move. That makes it hard to tell where the animal is looking.

To complicate matters, those same eyes also have big glassy lenses that had to be added after the animators had finished painstakingly adjusting the characters' eyelines. To everyone's surprise, the bending of light through those lenses changed the eyelines, creating hours of extra labor for ILM's exasperated artists and sending software technicians scrambling to compensate. The problem was especially troublesome with the Mariachi Owls, Ambrose, the Mayor, Sgt. Turley, and Buford.

Says visual effects supervisor John Knoll wryly, "We're starting to realize why nobody does deeply refractive eyes: because it's kind of hard." ☺

above: JIM BYRKIT ⬦ *Saloon Storyboard of Waffles*
right: ILM ⬦ *Final Renders*

THE LAY OF THE LAND

WHILE *RANGO* BEGAN with a simple concept—a Western with desert animals as the characters—it soon took on a life of its own. "It's always been important to me that the environment be treated as a character," says director Gore Verbinski. "When you wander through the desert long enough, it begins to speak to you. I wanted the audience to hear that voice."

"It's not photo-real," says animation supervisor Hal Hickel, "it's sort of photo-surreal."

The movie begins with its hero in a metaphorical womb: his terrarium, which seems deceptively safe. After a traumatic birth, he arrives in a world equally rich in wonder and danger. In the desert, says supervising art director John Bell, "the color, the lighting really gives a feeling like 'Man, this guy's world is upside-down.' He's in a spot where he shouldn't be."

The commitment to the surreal is apparent from Rango's Dalí-esque dream to the juxtapositions of Dirt. The latter has the familiar feel of a Western movie town, but beyond that, says production designer Crash McCreery, "we took liberties wherever we wanted to." Scale—as evidenced, for instance, by the enormous underground eye the posse passes in the cavern—was particularly free-form. "I never questioned a tire being the size of a skyscraper and then a porcupine standing next to a beetle that is the same size," says McCreery.

"We made the world the way we wanted to make it," he continues. "We took all of the elements of a desert and the animals of the desert and just created what we thought was the best world we could make to tell the story." ✪

left: JOHN BELL, CHRISTIAN ALZMANN & CRASH M^cCREERY ♣ *"Dysfunctional family. Needs intervention."*

RANGO'S TERRARIUM

---

*R*ANGO'S OPENING SEQUENCE IS A FACADE, EXPLAINS JOHN BELL, THE SUPERVISING ART DIRECTOR WHO SUPPLEMENTED THE DRAWINGS OF CONCEPT ARTIST JAMES CARSON AND ILLUSTRATOR JIM MARTIN. "[DIRECTOR] GORE [VERBINSKI] WANTS to give the impression that this is yet another CG-rendered film that looks a lot like the other films that have come to date: very safe, very candy colored, very smooth, very passive."

"It's a sucker punch," says Verbinski. "We played to the conventions of an animated film and then abruptly shattered them."

The terrarium set, in contrast to the rest of *Rango*'s world, is nearly free of wear and imperfections. "So the guitar looks pretty new," says Bell. "The sword looks pretty new . . . The tree is plastic, so it looks plastic. The sky behind him is very flat, almost two-dimensional, very graphic. We tried to maintain that 2-D graphic quality."

"The essential journey that Rango goes on," says writer John Logan, "is to find his home, to find the place he's meant to be. As he begins alone, his friends are a broken mechanical fish, a little palm tree, a headless Barbie doll. It's very sad in a way. But Rango has a great spirit. He wants to fill his world. He wants to fill his life with meaning and love. Because there's no one actually in his world, because he's in a sterile terrarium, he invests his affection in these inanimate objects, and they become the people he cares about. During the course of the movie, he meets other animals, other living people, and he finds the family where he's meant to be.

"And just to emphasize that in a way, to make him the most entertaining character we could, we just sort of embraced his theatrical character, that he loved the theater, and that he's an actor at heart. So initially, he's playing various parts for his inanimate object friends in the terrarium." ❂

right and opposite: ILM ↓ *Final Renders*

THE DESERT

AFTER THE TERRARIUM BREAKS ON THE SIDE OF A HIGHWAY, THE MOVIE SUDDENLY ACQUIRES RICH TEXTURES AND A MUCH EDGIER FEEL AS OUR STILL-NAMELESS HERO TREKS THROUGH THE DESERT. Concept artist James Carson says, "It was very important to make it look like a traditional desert, a very dry, inhospitable place, but at the same time try to incorporate some beauty and some starkness and some of the things that make a desert so appealing."

To get better compositions in the background along the desert highway, director Gore Verbinski would force the perspective, rearranging and resizing telephone poles in zigzags that would get any phone company engineer fired. Immediately, ILM began to realize how much "cheating" the filmmakers would need in order to create specific compositions. "On a film set, we move props and set dressings, pull walls—whatever it takes to build the frame," says Verbinski. "The demands on ILM were significant as everything changed from shot to shot." ✷

above: ILM ✷ *Final Render*
right: BRETT NORTHCUTT ✷ *Digimatte Painting of Desert Buttes*

THE TOWN OF DIRT

✦

DIRT HAS THE BONES OF A CLASSIC WESTERN TOWN IN THE SERGIO LEONE STYLE. "BUT HOW WOULD ANIMALS BUILD A SERGIO LEONE TOWN?" ASKS HEAD OF STORY JIM BYRKIT. "THEY WOULD SCAVENGE and rummage and find whatever they could out in the desert environment. So there are no ninety-degree angles to anything. Everything is a little rickety and janky looking."

Many of the buildings are made from human detritus. As it happens, concept artist James Carson's wife collects antiques, so some of Dirt's buildings are objects from his house. "The general store was a magazine rack I tipped upside down," he says. "The bank is an old steamer trunk in our living room."

Those visual puns are meant to be fun but not distracting, says production designer Crash McCreery. "You're looking at the character. You're looking at the environment. It feels like an old Western. You feel the heat. He's parched. And then you realize, 'Oh, the bar is a gas can—that's cool.'" ●

left: DAVID SHANNON ↴ *Original Ritual Concept*

UNDERTAKER

above: JAMES CARSON ✔ *Final Undertaker Concept*
below: EUGENE YELCHIN ✔ *Original Undertaker Concept*

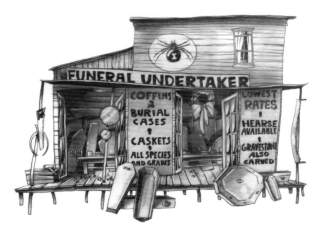

BARBERSHOP

left: JAMES CARSON ✔ *Final Barbershop Concept*
above: EUGENE YELCHIN ✔ *Original Barbershop Concept*

SALOON

left: EUGENE YELCHIN ⬦ *Original Saloon Concept*
above: JAMES CARSON ⬦ *Final Saloon Concept*

DENTIST

left: JAMES CARSON ↓ *Final Dentist Concept*
above: EUGENE YELCHIN ↓ *Original Dentist Concept*

BOOT STORE

above: JAMES CARSON ↓ *Final Boot Store Concept*
right: EUGENE YELCHIN ↓ *Original Boot Store Concept*

BANK

above: JAMES CARSON ↘ *Final Bank Concept*
left: EUGENE YELCHIN ↘ *Original Bank Concept*

BLACKSMITH

above: JAMES CARSON ↘ *Final Blacksmith Concept*
right: EUGENE YELCHIN ↘ *Original Blacksmith Concept*

GUN STORE

above: JAMES CARSON ⬇ *Final Gun Store Concept*
right: EUGENE YELCHIN ⬇ *Original Gun Store Concept*

GENERAL STORE

above: JAMES CARSON ⬇ *Final General Store Concept*
right: EUGENE YELCHIN ⬇ *Original General Store Concept*

CLOCK TOWER

above left: JAMES CARSON ↘ *Final Clock Tower Concept*

above right: EUGENE YELCHIN ↘ *Original Clock Tower Concept*

OUTHOUSE

above: JAMES CARSON ↘ *Final Outhouse Concept*

CANTINA

right: JAMES CARSON ↘ *Final Cantina Concept*

SUBTERRANEAN JOURNEY

★

HAVING CHOSEN A NAME AND ACQUIRED A BADGE, RANGO LEADS HIS POSSE ON AN UNDERGROUND JOURNEY IN SEARCH OF THE TOWN'S STOLEN WATER. SUPERVISING ART DIRECTOR JOHN BELL says, "That sequence was dictated by one image: [production designer] Crash [McCreery] had done one shot that has this giant eyeball and the characters' silhouettes as they walk in front of it. That just sets the tone for that whole sequence.

"[Director] Gore [Verbinski] wanted that sequence to feel like Carlsbad Caverns, where you walk into some of those rooms that just open up. You go from this very small tunnel area into this vast, vast cathedral of underground splendor." ✪

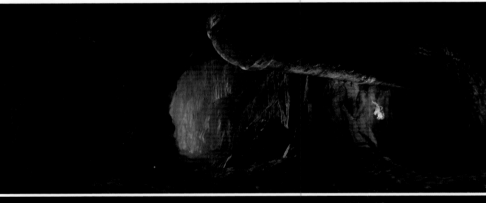

top left: CRASH M^CCREERY ↘ *Original Subterranean Journey Sketch*
top: JIM BYRKIT ↘ *Final Subterranean Journey Sketch*
above middle: JAMES CARSON ↘ *Final Tunnel Art*
above bottom: JAMES CARSON ↘ *Final Opening Art*

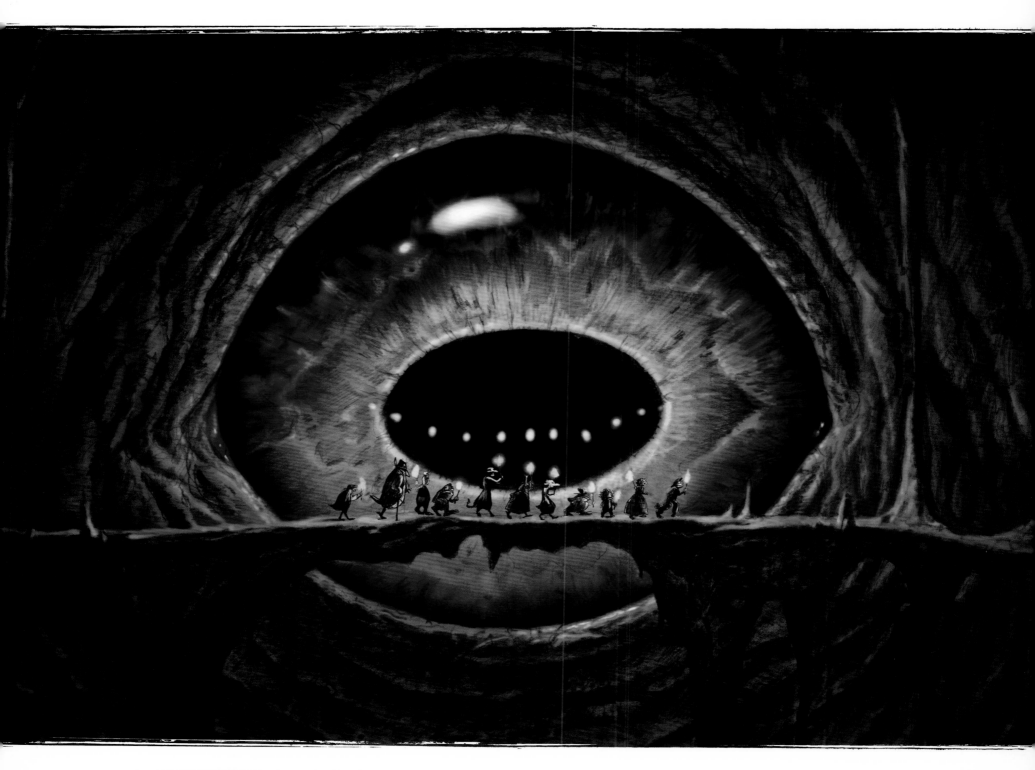

above: CRASH MᶜCREERY ❧ *Final Subterranean Journey Art*

THE APPLE BOX: LAYOUT & CAMERA

IT'S JUST AFTER NINE on a gray July morning in the Presidio, cool even by San Francisco standards. Past the statue of Yoda guarding the entrance and the *Star Wars* memorabilia in the lobby, in the bowels of ILM headquarters, visual effects supervisor John Knoll sits at the front corner of a crowded screening room, sipping coffee as artists present dailies. Looking at a shot from *Rango*'s watery climax, he notes odd reflections in a character's eyes. "It's a little *Village of the Damned*," he says.

Today, director Gore Verbinski and production designer Crash McCreery are "down south" in Los Angeles; they'll review footage by teleconference later. They are splitting their time between L.A., where the focus is on music, sound, and other tasks; and ILM, where they can work directly with the animators. "The distance is difficult," concedes McCreery. "There's something about that face-to-face time that's so important."

Even after animators have satisfied Knoll, McCreery, and Verbinski, the shots are far from finished. At this point, the sets are built and the actors are ready to perform, so to speak. But everything still must be lit and the camera still must be placed. "We're definitely really trying to get as much of a photographic look as possible," says visual effects supervisor Tim Alexander. "Our biggest challenge was to come up with a look that we knew would be unique, that people would want to look at for an hour and a half."

The difficulty of placing and blocking the virtual camera took ILM somewhat by surprise. Says animation supervisor Hal Hickel, "I think we underestimated—and I think this includes Gore, actually—how difficult it was going to be moving from the two-dimensional storyboards into the three-dimensional scenes." That transition is the province of the layout department, which sets up the virtual camera. On live-action films with visual effects, the layout department matches the camera moves of the original "plate," or live-action footage. ILM is quite expert at that. However, Hickel says, "What we didn't have was a really big, strong department of people who were just creating camera work from scratch." Verbinski and ILM's layout artists had trouble even communicating. Verbinski would ask for a lens and camera movements in the language of live production, but ILM's layout artists, used to talking about digital controls, didn't understand the jargon.

Even when they did find a common language, though, it wasn't enough. Verbinski's quest for texture and grit extended to *Rango*'s camera work. He wanted *Rango* to feel as if it had been shot with a physical camera, with human beings operating the machine. That meant deliberately adding subtle "noise" to the perfectly smooth movements a computer delivers.

Two of ILM's top layout specialists came on to help. Colin Benoit had worked on Michael Bay's movies; Nick Walker is a ten-year veteran of DreamWorks Animation who had recently joined ILM. As it turned out, even in his work on animated movies, Walker had never encountered quite the situation he faced on *Rango*. "The directors I'd worked with [at DreamWorks] are story artists who don't know the first thing about a camera. [Verbinski] knows everything about a camera, can

look at the storyboard and say, 'That feels like a twenty-seven-millimeter lens to me.' It's a much more particular sort of eye."

Walker felt, though, that doing layout after animation, as was done on *Rango*, was better than doing it during or even ahead of animation, as it was done at DreamWorks. Differences in a camera move as small as just a couple of frames, he says, can make a huge difference to the emotional impact of a shot. "So being able to wait until that animation is locked down is key to making the really subtle stuff."

Verbinski eventually sent his favorite live-action camera operator, Martin Schaer, to teach the ILM team his methods. Schaer even worked directly with a virtual camera (similar to what James Cameron used for all-digital shots on *Avatar)* to "shoot" some sequences in the final cut of *Rango*.

In time, Verbinski bonded with the layout team, as he likes to do with his live-action crew. "Gore is a camera guy," observes Benoit, "and he wants his camera operators with him.

That's how he works live-action. He works with Martin all the time." So Verbinski stuck to his live-action terminology, and the layout artists adjusted. "Instead of 'Move that character up in frame,'" says Benoit, "it would be 'Put that character on an apple box.'" Adds Walker, "We actually even wound up making a CG apple box prop, just as a joke, to put under characters out of frame."

One notable departure from typical animated movies: lots of close-ups. "Traditionally with animation," observes cinematographer Roger Deakins, who served as a consultant on *Rango,* "it's almost like you've done this animation, so you want to show it all. [But] with *Rango*, with the detail that they brought to the characters, you want to see it tight."

Producer John Carls sums up the relationship: "Gore has certainly gotten the best out of ILM, and I think ILM has certainly gotten the best out of Gore, meaning they've learned a lot from Gore. And that's been a joy to watch." ⚙

preceding pages: CRASH M^cCREERY & JOHN BELL ↴ *"No man can walk out on his own story."*
above: ILM ↴ *Final Render*

above: CRASH M^CCREERY ✦ *Romance*

LEAD ANIMATORS

AS ANIMATORS ARE THE ACTORS on an animated movie, it fell to animation supervisor Hal Hickel to cast the leads—that is, the lead animators. He chose Maia Kayser to head up the Beans team and Kevin Martel to oversee Rango.

"[Kayser] was kind of an obvious choice in that she's one of the very few women animators we have," says Hickel. "But she's also one of our very best animators. I knew Beans had to have somebody who was really at the top of their game."

Born in Argentina and schooled in Germany, Kayser says she's passionate about character animation. "You know, we communicate mostly with body language, and I love doing that, seeing how something comes alive from scratch, and suddenly you're giving something life."

Martel, an Ontario native, was an animator on several major franchises, including *Star Wars* Episodes I–III and the *Harry Potter* films. He was the first animator Hickel chose for *Rango*. "He has a great kind of dry sense of humor. Not too goofy. [Director] Gore [Verbinski] wanted a less-is-more approach to the humor, and Kevin is just the perfect guy for that."

Verbinski sums up working with them succinctly: "Kevin and Maia, they understand fuzz," he says. "With those great animators, you don't have to talk mechanics. You inspire them, and they perform." ☺

above: JIM BYRKIT ✵ *Vault Key Frame Art*
right: ILM ✵ *Final Renders*

"FUZZY" ANIMATION

DIRECTOR GORE VERBINSKI'S aesthetic commitment to "fuzz," or the imperfection of reality, would be most concretely realized in the animation phase as ILM set about putting the finishing touches on *Rango*'s look. Head of story Jim Byrkit's early art insisted on frayed clothing, errant hairs, rough stitches, and all manner of grime, grit, and sweat. Wood was mismatched from building to building. Hats had sweat stains and worn spots that would show if the light was right.

ILM's team soon realized how different *Rango* was from what they were used to. In 2009, a big visual effects movie might be one thousand shots, with six hundred of those having animation. *Rango* would be more than fifteen hundred shots, virtually all with animation. Most VFX work adds something (a spaceship, a dinosaur, a robot) to an existing plate. The plate arrives with its look already set, so the visual effect just has to fit in. On *Rango* there would be no plates. Every pebble, plant,

cloud, scrap of paper, and building would have to be designed and rendered from scratch.

Producer Shari Hanson explains that this process proved a bigger challenge than expected, even for seasoned VFX pros. "There's something about separating that live-action principal photography from the postproduction and visual effects part of it that allows you to internally compartmentalize the tasks at hand," she says. "But on an animated feature, it's just all one."

It helped that the ILM team had the same movies for reference that Verbinski had shown the team at the house: *Cat Ballou* for comedy, Sergio Leone and Sam Peckinpah Westerns for drama. The Leone influence, says production designer Crash McCreery, meant "grease, dirt, dust, sweat, something you don't normally see in a traditional animated movie. Landscapes are bleached and kind of desolate, so *Rango*'s bright green color plays against this desaturated environment." ☻

above: CRASH McCREERY & JOHN BELL ↓ *Pill Bug Golf*

LIGHTING

"WITH LIVE-ACTION," says layout supervisor Nick Walker, "you've got to light it in order to film it with a camera, whereas in computer animation, we can 'film it' as much as we want before we put a single light in there. The lighting can come afterward." That doesn't mean lighting is easy, though, especially in the context of *Rango*'s rough-edged aesthetic. To get the look of live-action lighting, director Gore Verbinski brought in cinematographer Roger Deakins, the regular director of photography for the Coen brothers and consultant on several computer-animated films, including Pixar's *WALL-E* and DreamWorks Animation's *How to Train Your Dragon*.

Deakins pulled dozens of reference images from both still photographs and old movies, ranging as far afield as *There Will Be Blood* and *Yojimbo*. ILM's lighting team would glean inspiration from the reference images, then send their work to Deakins for review.

Deakins's feedback soon revealed a philosophical difference between the VFX artists and the cinematographer. The artists tend to think in terms of simulating the natural world. For Rango's journey through the desert, explains visual effects supervisor John Knoll, that meant "a realistic sky, a realistic brightness of sun, and the right amount of balance from the sun beating on the ground. So on my first tests, I felt like, 'Wow, man, he really looks like he's in that hot desert environment.' And Roger's reaction was, 'Well, yeah, it feels a little too flat. What I'd do is I'd put a big black here to suck some

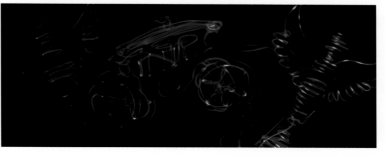

of that out and then put a bounce card over there to make it a little stronger and maybe a little bit of another card in the back to kind of rim him, to define that edge a little better.' I started to see what he was doing, and we started doing the visual equivalents of those."

Truth be told, live-action lighting is a poor simulation of reality. In a gunfight-in-the-street sequence, for example, it's typical for one gunfighter to be backlit. Logically, that would mean the other gunfighter would be frontlit. "In fact," says Knoll, "you've seen a million movies, and they never do that. You bring [the lighting] around so it's still attractive. You cheat all over the place." ⬢

right: CRASH MᶜCREERY ⬇ *Light Drawing*

COMPOSITING: PUTTING IT ALL TOGETHER

"COMPOSITING" HAS BECOME a very sophisticated art within visual effects. At its core, compositing means puzzling together the various pieces created by animators and set designers. Typically, computer-animated features rely on compositing less than visual effects movies. Animation studios prefer to create an entire scene, rather than piece it together, but VFX artists are used to compositing their effects into plates. ILM decided to use a lot of compositing on *Rango*, first because it was how they were used to working, but also because creating a scene in pieces meant that it would be easier to change an individual piece late in the game if need be.

Compositors added many of the finishing touches on *Rango*: dust, smoke, haze, heat ripple, and depth-of-field effects. "[Director] Gore [Verbinski] really likes atmospherics a lot," says visual effects supervisor John Knoll. "It's about

separating objects, creating depth by flattening contrast in the background."

Compositors also added a lot of Verbinski's fuzz. "We're also doing a process that we call 'film-tastic,'" says compositing supervisor Nelson Sepulveda, "which mucks it up and makes it look more like a piece of film: a little bit of chromatic aberration, a glint on the highlights."

Sepulveda's team added simulated film grain and the lens flares of the anamorphic lenses used for super-widescreen aspect ratios like *Rango's* (another unusual choice for an animated feature). Anamorphic lenses squeeze a wide image onto a narrow film frame and produce very distinctive horizontal flares when light hits them at odd angles. As anamorphic shooting has come back into vogue, ILM has become expert at reproducing those lens flares in its VFX. It brought that expertise to *Rango*.

above: ILM ↓ *Final Render*

CG CINEMATOGRAPHY

A CINEMATOGRAPHER MIGHT seem useless on a computer-animated movie, where expertise in cameras, lenses, and film stocks counts for little. But Roger Deakins says, "It's not about the hardware . . . A cinematographer brings his eye and his approach to his subjects, his way of expressing what he sees, just as a still photographer does. The personality is more important than the technology."

After lending his eye to several animated movies, Deakins sees a trend developing. "The digital-animated way of making movies has been kind of crashing, like moving plates, into the live-action way. Traditional animators are using live-action techniques, and the live-action filmmakers are taking techniques from animation to broaden their palette."

On *Rango*, Deakins says his contribution is "the juxtaposition between the brightness of the day exteriors and the darkness of the interiors, the feeling of some of the night work. I think it's discovering that look, which was the most important thing; all of us were working on finding the look of the film. And from that point, just bringing these images to fruition." ☺

above: DAVID LOWERY ⬦ *Campfire Key Frame*
right: ILM ⬦ *Final Renders*

KEY SEQUENCES

Echoing director Gore Verbinski, visual effects supervisor John Knoll says ILM decided to view its lack of experience in animation as a strength. "We're not coming in with any presuppositions about how animation should be. We're trying to take things that we're used to from our work on live-action and kind of apply those to the animated world." But visual effects work is generally done shot by shot. A plate arrives from principal photography, and the VFX artists add something to it and move to the next shot. For *Rango*, ILM's team had to focus on entire sequences at a time, so sequences were assigned lead animators, just as characters were.

They'd show their work to Verbinski in three phases, getting feedback at each stage: basic blocking, 75 percent complete, and then a final pass.

Andy Wong was lead animator on one of *Rango*'s most complex sequences, the posse's attempt to retrieve Dirt's stolen water and the riotous action sequence that follows. "[When] seeing dailies, honestly I can say every day we're laughing," says Wong. "Then seeing rendered stuff, the performance is great, and then visually it's great, and then the two things complement each other and bring it to this upper level. It's pretty cool." ✪

right and opposite: JIM BYRKIT ✧ *Pill Bug Journey Sequence*

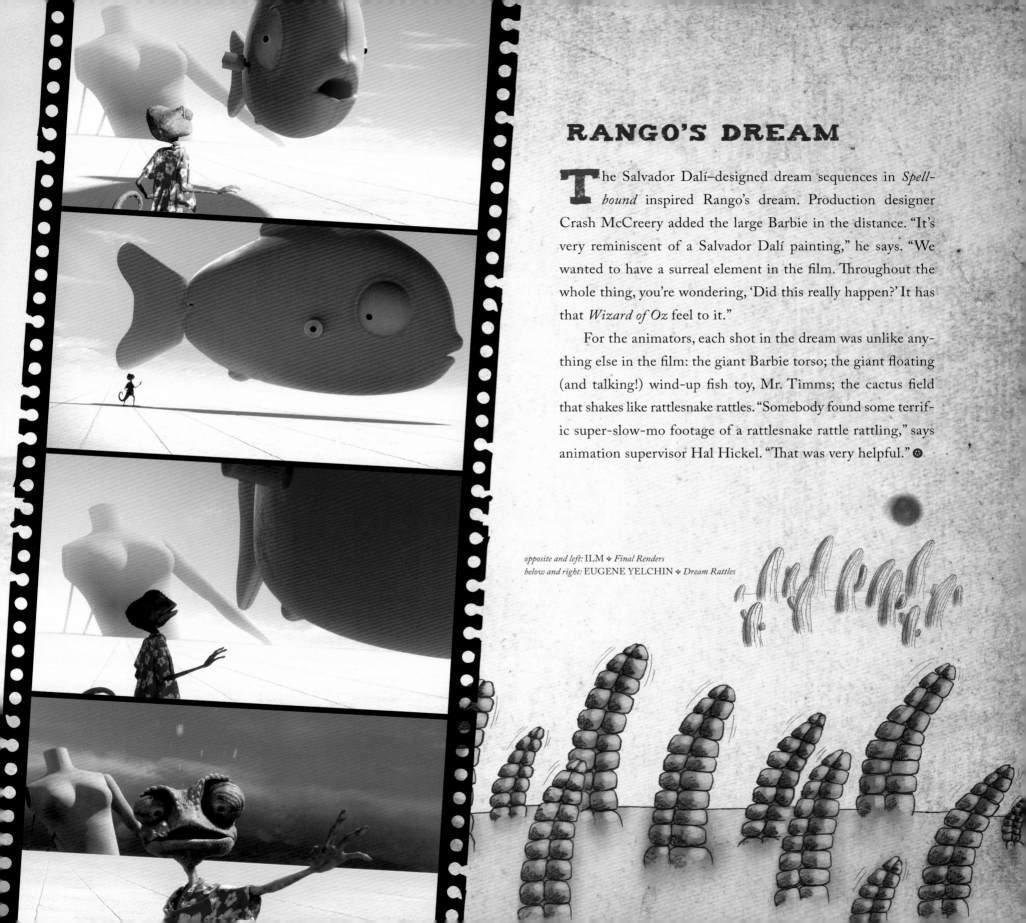

RANGO'S DREAM

The Salvador Dalí–designed dream sequences in *Spell-bound* inspired Rango's dream. Production designer Crash McCreery added the large Barbie in the distance. "It's very reminiscent of a Salvador Dalí painting," he says. "We wanted to have a surreal element in the film. Throughout the whole thing, you're wondering, 'Did this really happen?' It has that *Wizard of Oz* feel to it."

For the animators, each shot in the dream was unlike anything else in the film: the giant Barbie torso; the giant floating (and talking!) wind-up fish toy, Mr. Timms; the cactus field that shakes like rattlesnake rattles. "Somebody found some terrific super-slow-mo footage of a rattlesnake rattle rattling," says animation supervisor Hal Hickel. "That was very helpful." ✪

opposite and left: ILM ↓ *Final Renders*
below and right: EUGENE YELCHIN ↓ *Dream Rattles*

HAWK ESCAPE

In addition to the challenges of a frog with nearly perfect rock camouflage and the wings on a realistic hawk, Rango's Coke bottle refuge proved tricky. Animation supervisor Hal Hickel explains: "What looked to be a good size for the bottle when it's rolling along and Rock Eye is running alongside it tended to be much smaller than what we needed to put Rango inside it . . . When we made it big enough for him to run inside it, it was enormous. We play the bottle a different size in almost every shot, depending on what looked good." ⊙

above: DAVID SHANNON ↓ *Hawk Original*
right and opposite: ILM ↓ *Final Renders*

SALOON

Upon arriving in Dirt, hot and parched, Rango goes into the saloon for a drink and meets the ill-tempered townsfolk. By the time he leaves, he's lied about being a killer, gotten into a gun duel, and chosen a name: Rango. The legend is born.

The saloon is a critical sequence, as it's the entrance for many important characters. "The doors to the saloon act as a 'rabbit hole,'" says director Gore Verbinski. "Once he goes through them, Rango's entire perspective changes."

Rango's entrance into the saloon is the movie's first real interior scene, so it had to establish the movie's high-contrast look. The scene was devilishly difficult to light, says cinematographer Roger Deakins. "It's alright having an idea of the saloon being very dark and being lit by shafts of sunlight coming through the cracks in the walls and then bouncing off surfaces. Lighting in a computer that way is probably far more difficult than if you were doing it in live-action."

Supervising art director John Bell notes the length of the scene put pressure on the design team as well. "The shots were going to be slower, and, when you've got slow shots, you have to add a lot more detail. With that detail, you have a layer of richness. There's stuff piled up against walls and posts, and there are horseshoes and there are ropes. The upper deck off to the back of the saloon has clothing and blankets that have been draped over it. There's a lot of little fine details I think will be fun for the viewer to discover as they watch this film and hopefully rewatch it."

Verbinski's fondness for atmospherics put ILM to task in this sequence with its smoke and many shafts of light. "This is what ILM can do better than anyone," says Verbinski. "Scenes like this one are why it was so important to have them as a partner. The number of characters and difficulty of lighting actually shut down the entire facility. At one point, the entire capacity of the ILM render farm overloaded. I love doing that!" ☻

opposite and left: ILM ↓ *Final Renders*
following pages: CRASH McCREERY & JAMES CARSON ↓ *"To find water, you must find Dirt."*

SHOWDOWN / KILLING THE HAWK

Rango's duel in the sun with Bad Bill is a classic Western gunfight with a bit of Don Knotts layered in, but it's interrupted when the Hawk lands on Main Street, sending Bad Bill fleeing in terror. Recording this scene on the soundstage, actor Ray Winstone took Verbinksi's direction to add real physicality to his voice recording to heart. While delivering his lines, Winstone waddled to approximate the gait of a Gila monster standing upright, then nearly injured himself sprinting away. "I'm fifty-three years of age trying to run about like a young athlete. It just ain't there anymore, you know?" he laments. "I used to be a boxer, and I never got hurt so much as I did doin' this animation film."

When Rango flees the Hawk, he ducks into back alleys that weren't part of the original design. "A lot of the main street had been designed," says supervising art director John Bell, "and nobody had really started to touch the alleyway. So I took a stab at what the alleyway could look like, thinking that if the main street is supposed to be the nice part of town, then the back alley will be that much more chaotic." ◉

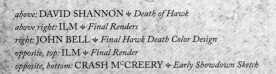

above: DAVID SHANNON ↳ *Death of Hawk*
above right: ILM ↳ *Final Renders*
right: JOHN BELL ↳ *Final Hawk Death Color Design*
opposite, top: ILM ↳ *Final Render*
opposite, bottom: CRASH MᶜCREERY ↳ *Early Showdown Sketch*

RODENT HIDEOUT

The sheer size of this sequence was daunting for everyone. One shot has around one thousand rodents, which were considered separate entities. Sequence lead animator Andy Wong says, "Because of the way they're interacting and the subtleties and stuff, we're doing brute force, we're animating every single character."

Among the challenges, he says, were "managing choreography and continuity, because the action is fast, but we are trying to showcase main characters and how they relate during the chase."

The sequence becomes even more complex when the rodents mount an aerial attack riding a squadron of battle-scarred bats. "It gives us a great mid-movie gigantic crazy action sequence," says animation supervisor Hal Hickel. "That was really super fun for the guys here, because while they were digging all the acting work, they were also itching to get into some really fun, kinetic action scenes."

"Early on in the story reel process, we knew we were headed for a classic shoot-out in the canyon, but it always felt static," says director Gore Verbinski. "We needed to get things moving, to add a little *Road Warrior* to the Western archetype. The bats were a solution that allowed us to create velocity, and to add aerial combat. They really opened things up. This was the only sequence in our story reel that was previsualized." ⊙

opposite: CRASH M^cCREERY & JIM BYRKIT ↳ *Bat Attack*
left: ILM ↳ *Final Renders*

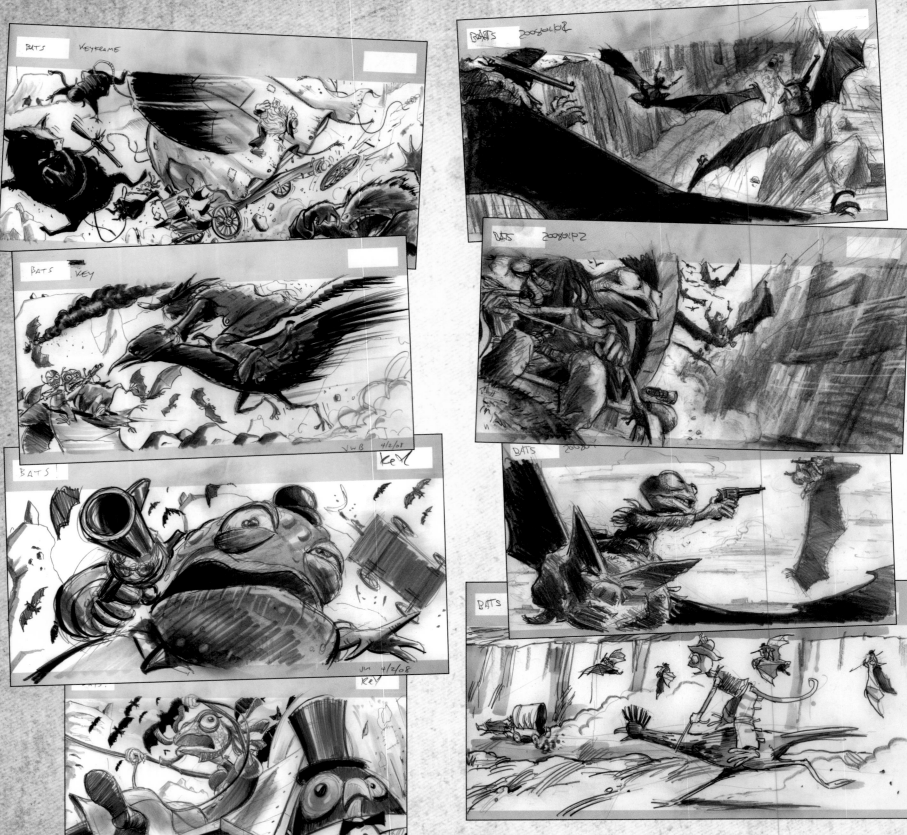

left: JIM BYRKIT ⬐ *Bat Chase Storyboards*
top: JOSH HAYES ⬐ *Bat Chase Storyboards*

opposite, bottom right and top left: DAVID LOWERY ✹ *Bat Attack Storyboards*
top right: JOHN BELL & CRASH MᶜCREERY ✹ *Bat Canyon*
above: CRASH MᶜCREERY & JOHN BELL ✹ *Bat Canyon*

RANGO VS. RATTLESNAKE JAKE

"Sooner or later, drama's about conflict, and you need the white hat and the black hat to go up against one another," says writer John Logan of Rango's final shootout with the bad guys. "It's all the tropes we've loved from every Western we've ever loved: *High Noon*; *The Good, the Bad and the Ugly*; *The Wild Bunch*. We put a little tip of the hat toward them, to make it the most exciting and classical scene that we could."

Lead animator Jakub Pistecky enjoyed the way the advantage was traded between the opponents in the constantly shifting battle between Rango and Jake. "It's a bit like a boxing match," he says. "Rango comes out strong, but Jake comes up short of the trap Rango's set for him, and that's a blow. Then Wounded Bird gets shot down, and that's a blow. There's a nice back-and-forth."

In this climactic showdown between sheriff and villain, Rango even earns a gesture of respect from Rattlesnake Jake, who sees in Rango the real hero the lizard only pretended to be in their first meeting. As writer John Logan points out, "all great heroes and villains . . . are different sides of the same coin if you write them well, and if they're presented in the right way. So it made perfect sense to me that Jake could look at Rango kind of as a kindred spirit." ◉

right and opposite: ILM ✧ *Final Renders*

RANGO'S EPIPHANY, CATHARSIS, RESURRECTION

Humiliated by Rattlesnake Jake, Rango comes full circle, returning to the desert highway where his quest began, even encountering Mr. Timms and the Barbie torso. Writer John Logan explains, "He has to ask himself the immortal question, which is, 'Who am I? I'm an actor who tried to be all these things, and it's not satisfying. Who am I really? And what's really important to me?' And that's what sends him into town for his final confrontation with the Mayor and Rattlesnake Jake." As production designer Crash McCreery observes, "He makes it to the other side. It's the end of a journey but the beginning of his identity, so to speak."

The scene became a favorite of all the animators. "There's so much feeling in that scene," says animation supervisor Hal Hickel, "and there's virtually no dialogue." Two keys to getting Rango right: his drooping tail and his rumpled costume, with shirttail untucked.

Hoping to move the look for this sequence away from the typical blue tint of movie night scenes, supervising art director John Bell showed McCreery a book of Frederic Remington paintings. "When Remington would paint night scenes, they would always have this kind of green glow to them," says Bell. McCreery loved the idea. Of the final render, Bell says, "It's really desaturated, but it has kind of this teal-greenish glow. It's really nice." ✪

opposite: CRASH MᶜCREERY ↓ *Dream Vision*
left: ILM ↓ *Final Renders*

CLIMAX

Once Rango and Beans uncover the truth about the missing water, they find themselves in a *Perils of Pauline*–style death trap, threatened with drowning at the hands of the Mayor and his henchmen. After all the hot, dusty, grimy scenes that came before, the climax brings a new challenge: lots and lots of water—no small thing in digital animation. As geysers erupt around town, the ground cracks, wagons and buildings are wrecked, everything gets wet, and rainbows appear. Dirt literally becomes Mud.

The sequence also shows Rattlesnake Jake in fear for the first time, as he faces death and then is tossed about by the geysers. Jake proved so hard for the animators to control in this scene that in some shots he's actually animated in two pieces, one with the head and the other with the tail. "Their seams are hidden, so they look like one snake, but there's two of them in there," says lead animator Jakub Pistecky. "On the technical side, it makes it really slow and really difficult for them, so they've been really, really trying to discourage us from using two snakes. But with some shots, we had to do it." ✪

above: JIM BYRKIT ↓ *Vault Key Frame Art*
right and opposite: ILM ↓ *Final Renders*

CODA

In the final scene, we revisit all the main characters (now in beachwear), and the movie gets its happy ending. Solving the riddle of Dirt's water and becoming sheriff of Mud marks the end of Rango's quest. At last he is the hero he imagined he was. "Person by person, decision by decision, joke by joke, adventure by adventure, he is able to finally end up with a family and a great sense of belonging," says writer John Logan.

"I think simplicity of narrative allows for complexity of emotion," says director Gore Verbinski. "We have a very simple tale of a guy who just wants to be loved and ends up pretending to be something he's not in order to feel accepted, and he has to learn that people are counting on him. These are not the inanimate objects of his terrarium. These are real people, and real friends have different needs, and indeed a hero doesn't exist in a vacuum. A hero exists really in the eyes of his audience."

But production designer Crash McCreery observes with a laugh that the joy is not quite unalloyed. "There is a tinge of 'Wow, everything is great, but things have changed in the town.' Their lifestyles have changed. As the Mariachi Owls say, 'Even as they abandon their dignity . . .' So there's a little bit of a question about how much good Rango really did." ✪

opposite: CHRISTIAN ALZMANN ↓ *Coda*
left: ILM ↓ *Final Renders*
above: JIM BYRKIT ↓ *Coda Concept Sketch*

CONCLUSION: A LITTLE MADNESS

*R*ANGO INSPIRED UNUSUAL passion among those who worked on it, from concept artists to actors to animators. The sense of camaraderie and collaboration developed at Rancho Rango permeated the entire production. "We didn't want to shine individually," says production designer Crash McCreery. "We wanted this project to succeed, just because we loved it so much and it was so weird." For ILM animators, the chance to create extended characters, work cheek by jowl with director Gore Verbinski, and simply spread their wings was a thrill. "I think I'm more pleased with this as a whole thing than anything else I've ever worked on," says animation supervisor Hal Hickel. "I really love the fact that this film is completely unique. On one level you could say, 'Oh, it's a talking-critter film and there's nothing more conventional than that.' But there's just really nothing else out there that looks like this film or feels like this film."

That may be the biggest appeal of *Rango* to the men and women who made it. Yet anything so adventurous is inherently risky. It's risky making an animated movie about a spiritual quest for identity, a sophisticated theme to which the stereotypical animation audience of tykes and tweens might not relate, and basing the story in the Western, a genre young viewers hardly know.

But risk pervaded the entire project, which is how Gore Verbinski wanted it. He wanted the movie to have a clear voice and certainly achieved that goal, if writer John Logan is any judge. "As much as any movie I've ever been involved with," says Logan, "and that includes Marty Scorsese with *The Aviator* or Tim Burton on *Sweeney Todd* or Ridley Scott on *Gladiator*, this is Gore Verbinski's vision. He had his hand on the tiller every second, and the spirit of *Rango* is the spirit of Gore Verbinski."

On his office patio in the valley, with another teleconference with ILM beckoning, Verbinski reflects, "I just try to make movies that I would like to see. I can't apply data research to that. Hollywood seems to be shrinking into a 'Run the numbers, here's what worked before, let's make more stuff like that mentality.' So fewer and fewer filmmakers are given the freedom to go running off into the field to ask, 'What about this path or that path?' And I think audiences want us to do that. So there has to be a little madness in your approach to things." ☻

above: CHRISTIAN ALZMANN ↳ *Hero Rango Color Design*
opposite: JIM BYRKIT ↳ *Hero Rango Sketch*

ACKNOWLEDGMENTS

ONE WRITER'S NAME goes on the book, but this writer had a support system second to none. At Insight Editions, my editor Jake Gerli provided patient guidance, Lucy Kee managed a blizzard of interview recordings, and Mary Ann Smith and Jean Brown turned those recordings into transcripts at a breakneck pace. Phyllis Ungerleider and Kirsti Payne of Paramount offered valuable feedback. Adam Cramer of Blind Wink and producer Shari Hanson answered my requests and responded to my interruptions without complaint, regardless of the thousand other things they might have been working on. Miles Perkins and Stephen Kenneally of Industrial Light & Magic gave me the best access an author could ask for, even while the film was deep in production. My particular gratitude to Helen Breitwieser, for finding this opportunity; and to Tim Gray and Steven Gaydos of *Variety*, for their encouragement and support.

Finally, my personal appreciation and love go, as always, to my family, especially Sue Ellen and Miranda, who were unfailingly patient as I spent 2010's summer nights, weekends, and vacation obsessing about an imaginary chameleon. ⚙

COLOPHON

Publisher: Raoul Goff
Art Director: Jason Babler
Designer: Barbara Genetin
Acquiring Editor: Jake Gerli
Managing Editor: Kevin Toyama
Production Manager: Anna Wan

In addition to all the people thanked above, Insight Editions would like to acknowledge the invaluable contributions of Risa Kessler and Brian Miller at Paramount Pictures, Morgan Feeney at Blind Wink, Mikayla Butchart, and Jan Hughes.

above: DAVID SHANNON ↓ *Original Bank Robbers Concept*